T0300330

Welfare and the Well-Being of Children

FUNDAMENTALS OF PURE AND APPLIED ECONOMICS

Fundamentals of Pure and Applied Economics is an international series of titles divided by discipline into sections. A list of sections and their editors and of published titles may be found at the back of this volume.

Welfare and the Well-Being of Children

Janet M. Currie
University of California, Los Angeles, USA

A volume in the Labour Economics section
edited by
Finis Welch
Texas A&M University, Texas, USA

Routledge
Taylor & Francis Group

LONDON AND NEW YORK

First published 1996 by Harwood Academic Publishers.

2 Park Square, Milton Park, Abingdon, Oxon OX14 4RN
711 Third Avenue, New York, NY 10017, USA

Routledge is an imprint of the Taylor & Francis Group, an informa business

First issued in hardback 2016

Transferred to digital Printing 2004

Copyright © 1995 by Taylor & Francis

British Library Cataloguing in Publication Data
Currie, Janet M.
  Welfare and the Well-being of Children. –
  (Fundamentals of Pure & Applied
  Economics, ISSN 0191-1708; Vol.59)
  I. Title II. Series
  362.7

  ISBN 978-3-7186-5624-0 (pbk)
  ISBN 978-1-138-16576-2 (hbk)

Contents

Introduction to the Series

Drawing on a personal network, an economist can still relatively easily stay well informed in the narrow field in which he works, but to keep up with the development of economics as a whole is a much more formidable challenge. Economists are confronted with difficulties associated with the rapid development of their discipline. There is a risk of "balkanization" in economics, which may not be favorable to its development.

Fundamentals of Pure and Applied Economics has been created to meet this problem. The discipline of economics has been subdivided into sections (listed at the back of this volume). These sections comprise short books, each surveying the state of the art in a given area.

Each book starts with the basic elements and goes as far as the most advanced results. Each should be useful to professors needing material for lectures, to graduate students looking for a global view of a particular subject, to professional economists wishing to keep up with the development of their science, and to researchers seeking convenient information on questions that incidentally appear in their work.

Each book is thus a presentation of the state of the art in a particular field rather than a step-by-step analysis of the development of the literature. Each is a high-level presentation but accessible to anyone with a solid background in economics, whether engaged in business, government, international organizations, teaching, or research in related fields.

Three aspects of *Fundamentals of Pure and Applied Economics* should be emphasized:

- First, the project covers the whole field of economics, not only theoretical or mathematical economics.
- Second, the project is open-ended and the number of books is not predetermined. If new and interesting areas appear, they will generate additional books.
- Last, all the books making up each section will later be grouped to constitute one or several volumes of an Encyclopedia of Economics.

The editors of the sections are outstanding economists who have selected as authors for the series some of the finest specialists in the world.

ix

Welfare and the Well-Being of Children

JANET CURRIE

University of California, Los Angeles, USA.

INTRODUCTION

In 1990, Americans spent more than $131 billion on federal programs aimed at poor families with children, much of it in the form of income transfers to parents. Yet despite these expenditures, one in five American children was in poverty in 1990, the same ratio as in 1965. Further, one in four families was headed by a lone woman, and 37% of these families were in poverty. Smeeding (1989) estimates that in 1986, welfare programs reduced the child poverty rate in the United States by only 1.9% compared to reductions of 7.4%, 6.4% and 20.5% in Australia, Canada and the United Kingdom, respectively.[1]

These shocking figures have led to a consensus that the welfare system is not working. As President Clinton put it during the recent Presidential election campaign, 'No one likes the welfare system as it currently exists...' (The White House, February 3, 1993). One survey found that 41% of Americans thought that too much was spent on welfare. Only 25% thought too little was spent. However, when the words 'assistance for the poor' were substituted for 'welfare' in the same survey, 64% favored more spending and only 11% said we should be spending less.[2] It seems that Americans want to help the poor but have lost faith in the power of the welfare system to do so.

Welfare is usually identified with Aid to Families with Dependent Children (AFDC), a program that provides cash transfers to predominantly female-headed families with children. The program has two goals: To provide a decent standard of living for children, and to encourage self-sufficiency of parents. The problem is that these goals conflict — cash transfers to

---

[1] See Hanratty and Blank (1992) for a more detailed comparison of the anti-poverty effectiveness of Canadian and US welfare programs.

[2] The survey was conducted by the National Opinion Research Center (NORC) in 1984 and is cited in Ellwood (1988).

families with children could eliminate child poverty, but not without discouraging parents from working.

As a result of this conflict, neither goal has been achieved. Combined AFDC and Food Stamp benefits are not high enough to raise families with children from poverty — in fact in most states AFDC benefits for a family of three are not high enough to cover the rent of a modest two bedroom apartment. Yet AFDC also fails to make work an attractive option. Poor mothers who work are docked a dollar of benefits for every dollar that they earn, and face the loss of Medicaid, Food Stamps, and other benefits that are tied to the receipt of AFDC.

Politicians of the right and left argue that a welfare system with AFDC as its centrepiece should be replaced by a system that emphasizes individual responsibility and accountability, and that targets scarce resources to meet specific attainable goals. This monograph shows that a restructuring of the welfare system along these lines has already begun, and has been quietly proceeding for at least the past 15 years. Programs like WIC (Supplemental Feeding Program for Women, Infants and Children) that target a specific service directly to children, and the Earned Income Tax Credit, which provides income transfers to the working poor, are among the fastest growing federal programs. At the same time, the real value of AFDC benefits has been allowed to erode.

The purpose of this monograph is to assess what we know and what we still do not know about the effects of these changes in the structure of federal programs on the children who are their primary intended beneficiaries. Part 1 focuses on technical material regarding program evaluation, measures of child welfare, and an overview of the welfare programs. Part 2 focuses on the evaluation of specific programs. The question posed throughout is whether programs that provide specific services directly to children, or provide cash transfers only to parents who exhibit 'desirable' behaviors such as being employed, are more effective that traditional cash transfer programs.

The evidence suggests that programs that provide specific services directly to children do provide greater benefits than programs that provide transfers to parents. Furthermore, the more narrowly targeted the benefit, the greater the measurable effect. This result suggests that either the effects of unrestricted cash transfer programs are too small and diffuse to be detected, or that parents do not value the services provided to children as much as the children themselves might if they were in a position to choose.

I would like to thank Vandy Howell for excellent research assistance. She not only created tables and figures but provided invaluable research assistance. I also thank Jodi Fingerman. Financial support from the National Science Foundation under grant number SES-9122640, and from the National Bureau of Economic Research's Olin Fellows Program is gratefully acknowledged. Finally, I would like to thank Duncan Thomas for many helpful comments and discussions, and for his permission to summarise our joint research in Chapters 5 and 8.

Part 1: An Overview of Methods, Measures and Programs

The three chapters in this section lay the groundwork for the analysis: Chapter 1 begins with a discussion of methods of program evaluation. The omitted variables, endogeneity, and selection biases that frequently complicate non-experimental evaluations are explained, along with many of the problems involved in conducting social experiments. The chapter also outlines several approaches that have been developed for dealing with these problems. All involve strong assumptions, and the methods are not equally suitable for all problems. It is important to choose assumptions that are plausible in the context of the problem to be addressed, and to check that the results are robust to changes in these assumptions.

Chapter 2 makes the point that child well-being is a multi-dimensional concept and discusses possible measures. Examples of data sets that contain these measures are given in the Data Appendix.

Chapter 3 provides an overview of the main federal programs that benefit children. The largest federal programs for children are AFDC, Food Stamps, and Medicaid. Expenditures on AFDC have fallen over time, expenditures on Food Stamps have risen somewhat, and expenditures on Medicaid have shot up due to the increasing costs of medical care. Since 1975, the fastest growing programs in terms of both caseloads and expenditures have been WIC and the Earned Income Tax Credit, which can be thought of as a transfer program for working parents. Head Start also showed rapid growth. These patterns demonstrate the shift away from unrestricted transfers in the form of AFDC payments and towards more restricted transfers and programs targeted directly to children.

1. METHODS FOR EVALUATING WELFARE PROGRAMS

Families on welfare are poor and likely to be disadvantaged in other respects. Hence, it should not be surprising to find that their children also tend to be disadvantaged. In fact, it is possible that a family's participation in a welfare program could increase the well-being of a child substantially, and still leave that child worse off than an average child. In order to isolate the effects of welfare programs on children, we need to control for all relevant differences in the backgrounds and characteristics of participants and non-participants.

The standard way to do this has been to control for observable differences, such as differences in parental education and income, using Ordinary Least Squares regression (OLS), a procedure that is available in virtually all statistical software packages (see Theil, 1971, for a discussion of the properties and potential biases of OLS). This procedure attempts to compare participants and non-participants who have the same observable characteristics.

OLS estimates of program effects will be unbiased as long as the mean of any unobserved variables (which make up the 'error' term) is zero, and as long as unobserved variables are not correlated with the observable characteristics included as explanatory variables in the regression. These are important limitations because even the most comprehensive data set is likely to omit some potentially relevant characteristics of the parent or child.

Suppose for example, that children in families on welfare are likely to attend inferior schools, and that the quality of school is unmeasured, or poorly measured. Assume also that welfare participation has no effect on test scores, but that scores increase with school quality. If we estimate an OLS regression of test scores on welfare participation and omit school quality, we may erroneously conclude that welfare participation has a negative effect on test scores because the estimated coefficient on the indicator for welfare participation will incorporate the negative effect of inferior school quality. This problem is referred to as omitted variables bias. Note that if school quality were not related to welfare participation, then omitting it would not cause any bias — only omitted variables that are correlated with program participation cause problems.

A related concern is that other key variables may be determined jointly with program participation and with the outcome in question. Such variables are said to be *endogenous*. For example, suppose we wish to determine the effect of AFDC participation during pregnancy on birthweight.

Good prenatal care is associated with higher birthweights, and women on AFDC may have access to better prenatal care because they are covered by Medicaid. However, if we include both AFDC participation and adequacy of prenatal care in our model of birthweight, we may erroneously conclude that only prenatal care affects birthweight. The problem arises because prenatal care is treated as if it were a fixed, pre-assigned variable, rather than a variable that is chosen by the mother and affected by AFDC participation.

A third problem arises when researchers try to make inferences about the effects a program would have on a broad population of participants using only information about people who are selected into the program. For example, broad bi-partisan support exists for extending the Head Start program to serve children in all poor families. If current enrollees were a random sample of all poor children, then we would generalize from their experiences to the population of all poor children.

However, faced with limited resources and discretion about who gets into the program, it is unlikely that program administrators will choose a random sample of all applicants: They may choose either to target their resources to the neediest children, or to target them to relatively better off children who are judged to be most likely to benefit. Once again, if we can observe the criteria that are being used to select children into the program, then we can control for these characteristics when evaluating program effects. But in most cases, it is likely that selections are being made using variables that researchers do not observe.

Given that we are unlikely to ever have data sets that include all of the relevant variables, a number of approaches have been developed to deal with the problems of omitted variables bias, endogeneity, and selection. These include social experiments, instrumental variables techniques, 'natural experiments', selection corrections, and fixed or random effects estimators. These approaches are not all equally suitable for all questions or data sets. The purpose of this chapter is to provide an overview that emphasizes the underlying assumptions, and possible pitfalls involved in the use of each technique. References are given in each section for those who wish to see a more technical treatment.

A. Experiments

In principle, the effects of welfare programs could be evaluated in the same way that we evaluate the effects of a new drug: by conducting a randomized experiment. People would be randomly assigned to a treatment group and a control group. Random assignment would insure that there were no systematic differences in either the observable or unobservable characteristics of the two groups. Hence, the effect of the treatment could be deduced by comparing the means of the two groups.

One might wonder why it is necessary to randomly assign treatment and controls? Why not find a group of similar people who are not in the program and compare them to the 'treatment' group? This procedure is sometimes called a 'quasi-experiment'. Lalonde (1986) shows that this strategy can produce very misleading estimates. He begins with data from a true randomized experiment, which means that he knows the effect of the treatment. He then draws several comparison samples who have observable characteristics similar to those of the people in the treatment group from publicly available data sets. He shows that comparisons of the treatment group with these artificial 'control' groups do not reproduce the experimental estimates. His examples highlight the importance of controlling for unobservables. Random assignment is critical to the success of an experiment because it ensures that people in the treatment and control groups will have similar observable and unobservable characteristics.

In practice, there are several problems that militate against the more widespread adoption of experimental methods. The first is cost. Heckman and Hotz (1988) report that one experimental evaluation of the Job Training and Partnership Act (JTPA) cost $20 million. Twenty million dollars is enough to fund a survey like the National Longitudinal Survey of Youth, which has been used to conduct many non-experimental evaluations, for 7 years.

A second problem is attrition from the sample. Large social surveys also suffer from attrition, but in experiments, attrition is likely to be greatest for those in the control group because they typically get very little out of participating in the experiment. Ashenfelter and Plant (1990) show that when there is differential attrition from the treatment and control groups, the assumptions one makes about those who leave the sample can have a great impact on the inferences drawn from the experiment — basically the remaining controls are likely to become less and less like the remaining treatments over time. Once one starts having to make assumptions about patterns of attrition, much of the attractive simplicity of the experimental approach is lost. Hence experiments may have little advantage over non experimental methods when it comes to evaluating the long-term effects of a program.

A third problem that afflicts experimental evaluations of welfare programs is the resistance of program administrators to the principal of random assignment. Many of these programs are entitlements, which means that anyone who meets the eligibility requirements is in principle entitled to participate. In practice, few programs serve all those who are eligible, but as discussed above, faced with budget shortfalls, most program administrators would prefer to target their services to those who are most in need, or to those who are likely to benefit most from the service.

The latter problem is particularly likely when administrators have to meet performance targets. Hotz (1990) reports that in August 1986, 73 JTPA sites were approached about participating in an evaluation and all refused because they were afraid that if they randomly assigned some applicants to be 'controls', their ability to meet performance targets specified by Congress would be impaired. (Ironically, the legislation that set the performance targets also mandated the experimental evaluations.) In the end, it was necessary to change the programs substantially in order to get sites to participate, and the resulting experimental programs were no longer representative of all JTPA programs.

In future, social scientists may respond to this problem, and to the problem of differential attrition from the control group, by taking a more flexible approach to the definition of controls. For example, in a drug trial, patients taking the new drug can be compared to those using an established drug. Since the effects of the established drug are known, the effects of the new drugs can be assessed without randomly denying treatment to needy people.

A fourth problem is that like a drug trial, a controlled experiment may give a lot of information of about how a particular intervention will work on a subset of the population under ideal, closely supervised conditions, but it may not shed much light on how a national program would operate.

Readers of the project evaluation literature should also be aware that not everything that is billed as an experiment involves random assignment. Some Head Start evaluations, for example, drew controls from lists of children waiting to get into the program. Lee *et al.* (1988) compared the treatments and controls from several Head Start evaluations and found that on average, the treatments had less educated mothers and were less likely to have a father-figure in the household than the controls.

Finally, given that there may be substantial heterogeneity between individuals, random assigment does not guarantee accurate results unless sample sizes are adequate. The problem is that in a small sample, one may

randomly assign all of the 'Type A' people to the treatment group and all of
the 'Type B' people to the control group. For example, Ashenfelter, Currie,
Farber, and Spiegel (1992), did a series of experiments aimed at determining the effect of various dispute resolution procedures on dispute rates. After a pre-test, they discovered that it was necessary to move to a much larger
sample than originally planned because otherwise the noise associated with
individual heterogeneity in dispute rates obscured the effects of the treatments.

In summary, although there is nothing more convincing than a well-de-
signed experiment with random assignment, there may be substantial problems associated with implementing experiments to evaluate welfare programs.[3] And there are many instances in which policy makers cannot wait
for the design and implementation of a social experiment. Non-experimental techniques offer quicker, cheaper, if ultimately less completely compelling answers.

B. Instrumental Variables, 'Natural Experiments', and Selection Corrections

Instrumental variables (IV) techniques are the non-experimental approach
most commonly used to address the problems of omitted variables bias,
endogeneity and selection. It is easiest to explain IV techniques in the context of omitted variables bias. Recall that the problem with the OLS estimate of the program effect was that it might be biased by the omission of
variables correlated with participation in the program. The idea behind IV
estimation is that it may be possible to find another variable or set of variables, known as instruments, that are correlated with program participation,
but uncorrelated with the omitted variables. A third requirement is that the
instruments must be variables that do not themselves belong in the equation
of interest.

If suitable instruments can be found, then the IV procedure can be implemented in two steps (see Theil (1971) for an introduction to IV estimation
and Bowden and Turkington (1984) for an in-depth discussion). Suppose
that the model we are interested in estimating can be written as:

$$Y = \alpha + \beta_1 P + \beta_2 X + \varepsilon, \tag{1}$$

where Y is the outcome we are interested in. P is an indicator equal to one if
the child is a participant in a welfare program, X represents a vector of

---

[3] See Hausman and Wise (1985) for a more detailed discussion.

other characteristics that affect outcomes, and ε is an error term that includes al unobservable variables. The problem is that some of the unobservable variables are correlated with both Y and P, so OLS estimation will yield biased estimates of the parameters, α, β_1, and β_2.

In the first step of the IV procedure, an OLS regression of program participation can be estimated in which P depends on both X and on the set of instruments, denoted Z:[4]

$$P = \gamma + \delta_1 X + \delta_2 Z + v. \tag{2}$$

The predicted probability of program participation, P^p, can then be computed using these estimates. This predicted value will not be correlated with the omitted variables since neither X nor Z are.

The second step consists of substituting the predicted probability of program participation for the actual value in equation (1):

$$Y = \alpha + \beta_1 P^p + \beta_2 X + \varepsilon. \tag{3}$$

The OLS standard errors must be adjusted to account for the fact that one is using a predicted rather than an actual value. Any standard statistical software package will produce the correct IV estimates and standard errors. Endogenous variables can also be instrumented as long as there is at least one instrumental variable for each endogenous one.

There are two problems that bedevil IV estimation. The first is that it is often extremely difficult to find instruments that are correlated with program participation, but uncorrelated with the omitted variables. Suppose for example, that we wish to estimate the effect of Medicaid participation on birthweight. In order to do so using IV methods, we need to find a variable that is correlated with Medicaid participation, but does not affect birthweight. It should be evident that characteristics of the mother such as education and marital status are unlikely to meet the latter criteria although they may well be correlated with participation in Medicaid. The use of invalid instruments can result in extremely inaccurate estimates of program effects.

One promising approach involves using state-level variation in the Medicaid program to predict participation. As discussed in Chapter 3 below, the Medicaid program is a health insurance program for the poor with

---

[4] Heckman and MaCurdy (1985), and Newey (1987) show that it is consistent and actually more efficient to use OLS (i.e. a linear probability model) in the first stage rather than a logit or probit model.

eligibility criteria that vary greatly from state to state. State-level measures
of program generosity are like to affect Medicaid participation, but are unlikely to directly affect birthweights unless many pregnant women move in
order to take advantage of generous Medicaid programs, or unless the generosity of state Medicaid programs is correlated with omitted characteristics of the state that affect birthweight, such as the availability of prenatal
care services. Often it is possible to include an indicator variable for each
state to control for any fixed characteristics of the state that may be important.

Studies that use state characteristics as instruments for individual decisions are often referred to as 'natural experiments'. The idea is that if state
characteristics are really unaffected by individual decisions, then people
can be thought of as being randomly distributed across treatment and control groups as in a real experiment.

Under these assumptions, state characteristics satisfy the criteria that the
instruments are variables that do not belong in the main equation. However,
it is often the case that these variables do not explain much of the variation
in program participation once individual characteristics have been controlled for. In this case, the results obtained using IV estimation are likely to be
pretty uninformative — the problem is that the predicted probability of program participation we are using in the second step, is not a very good prediction.

This problem is illustrated in Table 1. The first column contains OLS
estimates of the effects of Medicaid coverage on the number of doctor visits
for illness in a white U.S. child's first year of life. The OLS estimates
indicate that children with Medicaid coverage get almost half a visit more,
on average. The second column shows the IV estimates. The instrument list
includes the state's income eligibility threshold for Medicaid coverage, which
has a significant effect on the probability of Medicaid coverage (the t-statis-
tic is close to 4).[5] In addition, the R-squared of the first stage regression is
.26. Nevertheless, the point estimates generated by the IV procedure are
negative and the standard errors are so large, that we cannot reject either the
null hypothesis that the IV estimate is the same as the OLS estimate, or the

---

[5] Other instruments included county-level measures of AFDC payments per capita and
Medicaid payments per capita, state-level measures of these two variables, the number of
AFDC recipients per 1000 state residents, the number of Medicaid recipients per 1000 state
residents, and the percent of state Medicaid payments made to dependent children under 21
years of age. None of these variables were individually statistically significant in the first
stage regression.

TABLE 1
Medicaid and Number of Doctor Visits For Illness in the First Year

	OLS	TSLS
Interception	2.249	3.220
	(2.058)	(5.373)
Medicaid in	0.470	-0.165
Birth Year	(0.240)	(1.997)
Mother Characteristics:		
Permanent Income	0.205	-0.004
	(0.171)	(0.493)
Poverty Sample	-0.119	-0.162
	(0.179)	(0.203)
Top Grade in 88	0.013	0.016
	(0.051)	(0.053)
AFQT Score	0.200	0.152
	(0.311)	(0.370)
Urban at Age 14	-0.020	0.047
	(0.137)	(0.204)
Child Characteristics:		
Male	-0.309	-0.260
	(0.157)	(0.161)
Age in Months 1988		
13-36 months	0.745	0.781
	(0.305)	(0.352)
37-60 months	-0.372	-0.327
	(0.263)	(0.307)
61-84 months	-0.361	-0.362
	(0.240)	(0.250)
Community Characteristics:		
County per	-0.042	-0.033
capita Income	(0.064)	(0.065)
# Doctors per	-0.026	0.060
1000 State Resid.	(0.272)	(0.234)
# Hosp. Beds per	-0.231	-0.133
1000 State Resid.	(0.116)	(0.128)
State Infant	-0.062	-0.046
Mortality Rate	(0.074)	(0.077)
Northeast	0.620	0.509
	(0.323)	(0.373)
South	-0.91	0.106
	(0.300)	(0.312)
West	0.482	0.441
	(0.228)	(0.335)
R-Square	0.026	0.022
# obs.	2327	2272

Notes: Standard errors in parentheses.
Source: National Longitudinal Survey's Child-Mother File.

null that it is zero. This is the sense in which the IV estimates can be uninformative.

Nelson and Startz (1990a, b) give an example in which the IV 'cure' is not only uninformative but 'worse than the disease.' They show that when the instruments explain little of the variation in the endogenous variables it is possible in some instances to produce estimates that are not only severely biased but that appear to be precisely estimated.[6]

Instrumental variables techniques can also be used to deal with measurement error. Up to this point, the discussion has implicitly assumed that program participation is measured without error. However, when survey responses are compared to administrative records one typically finds underreporting of program participation (c.f. Marquis and Moore, 1990). One reason for under-reporting is that respondents simply forget spells of welfare receipt that occurred further in the past.

The effect of measurement error is typically to bias the estimated OLS coefficient on program participation toward zero. Suppose that program participation is actually positively correlated with the outcome of interest, but that it is badly measured and the measurement error is not correlated with the outcome. The OLS coefficient will be, in effect, a weighted average between the true positive correlation and zero, and hence will be biased towards zero.

Given an instrument that is not measured with error, it is possible to get an unbiased estimate of the effect of program participation by doing IV. As usual, the instrument must be correlated with program participation and uncorrelated with any omitted variables.

A final application of the instrumental variables technique involves the computation of 'corrections' for sample selection. To take up the example of selection outlined above, suppose that administrators choose the most disadvantaged eligible children to participate in Head Start. Then the OLS estimates of the effect of Head Start participation on the test scores of sample children will be an underestimate of the effect that Head Start participation would have on the test scores of the average eligible child. If we can find an instrumental variable that predicts selection into the program but has no effect on test scores, then we can use a two-step procedure pioneered by Heckman (1974, 1979) and Lee (1982) to 'correct' the OLS estimates

---

[6] (Bound et al. (1993) and Staiger and Stock (1993) also make this point.)

for the fact that some children are more likely than others to be selected into the program.

Following Heckman (1979), we can divide the problem into two parts:

$$Y = \beta_1 X_1 + \varepsilon_1 , \text{ and} \qquad (3)$$

$$P = \beta_2 X_2 + \varepsilon_2 . \qquad (4)$$

Equation (3) is the equation of interest, while (4) describes selection into the program. The problem with OLS estimation of (3) is that one of the conditions necessary for consistent OLS estimates of β_1 is violated: The fact that these children will score lower on standardized tests than other children with similar observable characteristics, is simply another way of saying that the mean of ε_1 is less than zero.

This problem can be solved by dividing the error term into a component that is due to selection, and a new random error term. Heckman shows that an estimate of the selection component of the error term can be derived from estimates of the selection equation (4). Equation (4) is usually estimated using a probit technique.[7] The estimates of β_2 can then be used to form the selection component (sometimes called the inverse Mill's ratio):

$$\lambda = f(-\beta_2 X_2/\sigma_2) / [1 - F(-\beta_2 X_2/\sigma_2)], \qquad (5)$$

where f denotes the normal density function, F is the cumulative normal density function, and σ_2 is the variance of the error term ε_2 .

Consistent estimates of β_1 can then be obtained via OLS estimation of:

$$Y = \beta_1 X_1 + \gamma_2 \lambda + v_1 . \qquad (6)$$

The significance of λ provides a test of the importance of selection.

Ideally, the vector X_2 in the selection equation (4) should contain some variables that are not in X_1. Otherwise, λ is just a non-linear combination of the variables in X_1, and identification depends on the fact that (4) was estimated using a non-linear technique. The main difficulty involved in estimating this type of model is that it is hard to find variables that explain selection into the program but do not affect outcomes.

---

[7] A probit is a technique suitable for zero-one dependent variables. A sketch of limited dependent variables models such as logits and probits is beyond the scope of this monograph, but see Maddala (1983) for a discussion.

C. Fixed Effects and Random Effects Models

Given repeated observations of siblings or of the same child, we can adopt a very different approach to the problem of omitted variables. Suppose for example, that we have a sample of children that includes more than one child per family. Then we can model their outcomes as:

$$Y_{ij} = \alpha + \beta_1 P_{ij} + \beta_2 X_{ij} + (v_{ij} + u_j). \tag{4}$$

where i=indexes the child, and j indexes the family. The error term has been divided into a component, v_{ij}, that is specific to each child, and a component, u_j, that is shared by all children from the same family. This shared component will include common aspects of the children's upbringing and genetic endowment. It is easy to see that if we transform the data by substracting out the mean for each family, the common component u_j is eliminated and the model becomes:

$$Y_{ij}' = \beta_1 P_{ij}' + \beta_2 X_{ij}' + v_{ij}', \tag{5}$$

where a prime indicates that the variable is measured in deviations from the family-specific mean. This procedure is algebraically equivalent to including a dummy variable, or 'fixed effect' for each family. If the omitted variables that are causing bias are constant within families, then they can be eliminated using this fixed effects technique (see Hsiao, 1986).

However, it is possible that there are omitted variables associated with the individual child that affect estimated program effects. Suppose for example, that a mother only enrolls her favorite child in Head Start. In this case, higher test scores on the part of the Head Start child could reflect maternal favoritism rather than an effect of Head Start *per se*. Given repeated observations of the same child, this source of bias could be addressed by including a fixed effect for each individual child rather than for each family.

This last example illustrates one of the limitations of the fixed effects methodology — unobserved characteristics that vary within the family or that change over time for the same child could also be important. A second problem is that focusing on families with more than one child or on children who are observed more than once may induce sample selection bias. For example, women who began families at younger ages might be more likely to have had more than one child by any given age than other mothers. Fixed effects estimates may also be biased towards zero by measurement error. The problem is that differencing may result in 'throwing the baby out with the bath water', since the true 'signal' may be discarded while the 'noise' remains. For example, if the child's age-adjusted IQ is the same at two points in time, but is measured with some error then taking the difference between the two IQ scores will leave only the error, which is unlikely to be correlated with program participation.

Finally, fixed effects estimates may be quite inefficient. In a data set with 3000 mothers and 2 or 3 children per mother, putting in a dummy variable for each mother would exhaust 3000 degrees of freedom. If for example, we knew that these mother-specific effects were normally distributed and that they were uncorrelated with the other explanatory variables included in the model (in which case the OLS estimates would be unbiased), then instead of estimating 3000 separate effects, we could estimate the mean and variance of the component of the error term associated with the mother-specific effects and use these estimates to improve on the efficiency of the OLS estimates. This is the idea that underlies random effects estimation (See Hsiao, 1986). However, in many applications, the assumption that the mother-specific effects are orthogonal to the other explanatory variables is unappealing.

D. Summary

In summary, the potential for omitted variables bias, endogeneity, and selection is likely to complicate any non-experimental assessment of program effects. This chapter outlines several approaches that have been developed for dealing with these problems. It is important to choose assumptions that are plausible in the context of the problem to be addressed, and to check that the results are robust to changes in these assumptions.

Finally, the fact that the potential for various biases exists does not necessarily mean that they are empirically important. In Chapter 5 we continue the discussion of the Medicaid example given above, and show that the estimated effect of Medicaid coverage on the number of doctor visits for illness is remarkably similar whether it is estimated by OLS or by including a fixed effect for each child. This finding suggests that people are selected into the Medicaid program largely on the basis of observable characteristics like race and income and the biases due to omitted variables are small once these observables are included in the model.

2. MEASURES OF CHILD WELL-BEING

Nothing could be more straightforward than to ask whether welfare programs benefit children. Yet once this question has been posed, it becomes
necessary to think about how benefits should be measured.[8] This chapter
discusses some common measures of child well-being. The multiplicity of
measures stems from the fact that well-being is a multi-dimensional concept and raises another difficulty: What is the most appropriate measure of
the effect of a program like AFDC, for example? Or, granting that health
status is the best measure of the effect of the Medicaid program, what is the
best measure of a child's health status? In the absence of hard answers to
these questions, the best strategy is likely to involve examining a broad
range of outcomes.

Table 2 provides an overview of the outcomes discussed in this chapter
and provides some examples of data sets that include information about
each measure. For convenience, the measures are divided into four broad
categories: Measures of health status, measures of test scores and academic
attainment, long-run measures of social competency, and other measures.
Further information about specific data sets is given in the Data Appendix.

A. Measures of Health Status

(i) Mortality

Infant and child mortality rates are perhaps the most objective and least
controversial measures of children's health status. The infant mortality rate
is defined as the number of babies born alive who die before reaching the
age of 1. At 10 per 1000, the US infant mortality rate (IMR) is higher than
that of most other industrialized countries (Danzinger and Stern, 1990).
African-American infant mortality rates are twice as high as white rates in
the US, and even the white infant mortality rate of 9 per 1000 exceeds the
IMR of most western European countries, Canada, Japan, Hong Kong, and
Singapore. After the first year, death rates fall sharply to 49 per 100,000
among children aged 1 to 4, and to 25 deaths per 100,000 among children 5
to 14. Death rates rise again to 100 per 100,000 for adolescents and young
adults (15 to 24) (US House of Representatives, 1992).

---

[8] Korenman and Miller (1993) suggest that long-term poverty has a greater impact than
short spells, which indicates that when benefits are measured timing may also be important.

TABLE 2
Publicly Available Data Sets with Measures of Child Well-Being

Data Set[1]	Measures
Nutrition and Health Measures:	
Owen's PNS (1968-70)	Eating habits, current dietary intake, medical history, biochemical evaluations, physical and dental evaluations.
TSNS (1968-70)	Dietary recall, socioeconomic status, physical and dental evaluations, biochemical and anthropometrical assessments.
NHANES I (1971-74)	24-hour dietary recall, sociodemographic data, health history, physical examination; anthropometric, hematologic, and biochemical measures.
NHANES II (1976-80)	24-hour dietary recall, sociodemographic data, health history, physical examination; anthropometric, hematologic, and biochemical measures, use of medication and dietary supplements.
HHANES (1982-84)	24-hour dietary recall, sociodemographic data, health history, physical examination; anthropometric, hemotologic, and biochemical measures. Participants were all Hispanic.
NDB (ongoing)	Nutrient data, nutritional composition of foods.
NFCS-LI (1977-78)	Household: Money value of food used at home, nutrient availability over a 7-day period, food stamp participation, socioeconomic status, family size. Individual: 3-day dietary intake.
SFC-LI (1979-80)	Household: Money value of food used at home, nutrient availability over a 7-day period, food stamp participation, socioeconomic status, family size. Individual: 24-hour dietary intake.
CSS (1980)	Students: current and past participation in food programs, availability and use of alternate food services, 24-hour dietary recall, anthropometric and socioeconomic characteristics.
HSP (1980)	Families: household composition, family economic status, family food expenditures.
FAS (1981)	Administrators: district and school characteristics, institutional and aggregate student participation in food programs, food service characteristics, meal prices, attitudes toward school food services.
NFCS-CSFII (1985, 1986, 1989)	24-hour dietary recalls (repeated at 2 month intervals; up to 6 measures per respondent), food stamp participation.
NFCS (1987-88)	Household: Money value of food used at home, nutrient availability over a 7-day period, food stamp participation, socioeconomic status, family size. Individual: 3-day dietary intake.
CDC-PNSS (1983, 1986)	Anthropomitric, hemotological results for children enrolled in public programs.
PSID (1968-present)	Annual food consumption, doctor visits, food stamp participation, disability of children, socioeconomic factors.

SIPP (1984-present)	Child's eating habits, mental state, and physical, emotional and mental disability status, child care arrangements and method of payment, socioeconomic factors.
CPS (1968-present)	Food stamp participation, school lunch participation, immunizations, welfare status.
VSCP (1968-present)	Infant mortality, prenatal care and birthweight, birth rates, teenage and unmarried births, family formation and dissolution.
Linked Birth/Infant Death Program (1983-1986)	Infant mortality rates by birth cohort, infant mortality rates by birthweight.
NNS (1964-66, 1967-69, 1972, 1980)	Birthweight, gestation length, birth length, number of prenatal visits to doctor, socioeconomic information about mother and father.
NMIHS (1988)	Birthweight, gestation length, adequacy of prenatal care, source of payment for care, WIC participation, illnesses, vaccinations, socioeconomic information about mother.
NHIS (1969-90)	Acute and chronic conditions, illness, injuries and associated disabilities, visits to physicians, dentists and hospitals; socioeconomic characteristics. Yearly current topics include health insurance information, child health, and health promotion.
NHIS-CH (1988)	Accidents, injuries, and medical conditions; birth weight and prenatal care; developmental, learning, emotional, and behavioral problems; school attendance; medical care, and health insurance.
NSFG (1973, 1976, 1982, 1988)	Prenatal medical care, pregnancy outcome, breast feeding, socioeconomic characteristics, child care, measures of mother's behavior between pregnancies, response to whether child was "wanted" or not.
NLSCM (1986, 1988, 1990, 1992)	Physical, emotional and/or mental conditions; accidents or injuries, hospitalization, Medicaid participation, anthropometric measures.
NSHSPE (1981-1982)	Type, severity and disposition of problems treated at schools; nurse practitioner's findings from medical histories and physical examinations of students, data on individual health care episodes at school, socioeconomic characteristics.

Education/Testing Measures:

NLSM (1986, 1988, 1990, 1992)	AFQT score of parents, reading and mathematics test scores, Head Start participation, other types of preschool participation, achievement on various tests of motor and social development, grade repetition, remedial education.
PSID (1968-present)	Educational level, parental expectations of educational level.
CPS (1968-present)	School enrollment, educational attainment.

NAEP (1970-1980)	Test results designed to reflect the knowledge, skills, understandings and attitudes of young Americans, socioeconomic factors. Individual and community level data.
HSB (1980, 1982, 1986)	Student: scores on a battery of tests including vocabulary, reading, mathematics, science, writing, civics, spatial orientation, and visualization; educational aspirations, job aspirations, personal values, grades. High school principals: school attributes and programs. Teachers: teacher evaluations of student. Parent: sibling files, socioeconomic characteristics, job expectations and educational expectations.

Other

NLSCM (1986, 1988, 1990)	Child care costs, Behavior Problems Index (BPI), self esteem of child, how many books child has, how many toys child has, organization membership, how often child eats meal with family, parents perceptions about child, family lifestyle.
NLSY (1979-present)	Teenage schooling attainment, fertility, delinquency, drug use, attitudes, employment histories, AFQT scores, family structure, aspirations.
PSID (1968-present)	Child care costs, neighborhood characteristics, wantedness of children.
CPS (1968-present)	Child care costs, child support payments.
CES (1979-present)	Annual food expenditures, preschool and nursery school enrollment and expenditures, health care expenditures, education expenditures, socioeconomic characteristics.
MF-CSLVY (1976-89)	Drug use, values, lifestyle orientations, socioeconomic characteristics.
NYS (1976-80)	Drug use, parental discipline, disruptive events occuring in the home, community involvement, neighborhood problems, socioeconomic characteristics.
NSC (1976, 1981, 1987)	Measures of child's well-being, experiences with family disruption; behaviour, physical and mental health.
NCS-CSS (1989)	Types of violence in school; general violent crime; personal larceny crimes; school attendance, type of school, distance from home; socioeconomic characteristics.

Notes: See the Data Appendix for a brief description of these data sets.

Although these rates are high by international standards, the numbers indicate that infant and child deaths are rare events, which means that very large sample sizes would be required to identify relationships between the generosity of welfare programs and death rates. Typically, data sets large enough to have many deaths have little background information about the child's family, so it is often difficult to implement the kind of estimation procedures discussed in the previous chapter. However, deaths from trauma appear to account for much of the disparity between the child mortality rates of rich and poor (Wise and Meyers, 1988). This suggests that patterns in serious accidents may be closely related to patterns in mortality, as well as being easier to identify because accidents are more common.

Users of IMR data should be aware that the difference between African-American and white rates persists at all levels of income (Reis, 1990). There is a long-standing debate in the health literature about whether this differential reflects physiological differences or environmental factors such as stress and residential segregation (Cramer, 1987). It is also true that Hispanics tend to have lower IMRs than would be expected based on their socio-economic characteristics, and that this ethnic differential is not well understood (Forbes and Frisbie, 1991). Given these unexplained differentials, it is advisable to stratify samples by race and ethnicity.

Finally, technological innovations such as the development of new procedures for ventilating premature babies can lead to rapid reductions in the IMR over short periods of time. Hence, one must be careful to control adequately for these changes.

ii) Birthweight

Birthweight is a second relatively objective measure of infant health. Children who are of low birth weight (medically defined as less than 2500 grams) are at higher risk of mortality and of lifelong disabilities such as cerebral palsy, autism, and mental retardation (McCormick *et al.*, 1992). In 1980, low birth weight infants accounted for less than 7% of all births, but 60% of all infant deaths (US House of Representatives, 1992). Schwartz (1989) reports that although babies weighing less than 2500 grams account for only 9% of neonatal hospital caseloads, they account for 57% of the cost of neonatal hospital care. The risk of death and disability is even higher among children of very low birth weight, which is medically defined as less than 1500 grams or 3.5 pounds.

Ideally, birthweight should be adjusted using gestation: A 4-lb. baby born after 7 months is likely to have a better chance of survival than a 4-lb. baby born after 9 months. This differential reflects the fact that, conditional on gestation, the 7-month baby has shown normal growth, whereas the 9-month baby is underweight for its gestational age. Babies who are small for

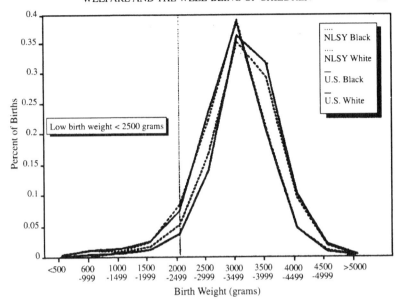

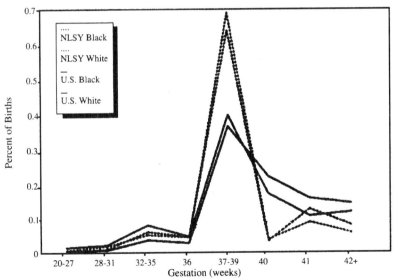

Source: Vital Statistics of the United States, Dept. of HHS, 1985.
National Longitudinal Survey of Youth, 1979-1985

FIGURE 1   Distribution of Live Births, NLSY Sample & US Population by Birth Weight and Gestation. Horizontal bar indicates 2500 grams.

gestational age have also been shown to suffer from impairments to their immune system that can persist from months to years after birth (Chandra, 1986).

However, in many surveys, gestational age is subject to a great deal more measurement error than birthweight. Figure 1 shows that in the National Longitudinal Survey of Youth (NLSY), for example, the distribution of gestational age is much more sharply peaked than it is in Vital Statistics data. In contrast, the distribution of birthweights in the NLSY is very similar to Vital Statistics data. The fact that spikes in the reported distribution of gestational age occur even in Vital Statistics data reflects the inherent difficulty involved in accurately determining the date of conception.

Many of the caveats that apply to IMR data also apply to birthweights. For example, although the effects of birthweights are highly non-linear, there are relatively few children of low or very low birthweight, so many researchers have chosen to treat birthweight rather than low birthweight as the outcome of interest (cf. Rosenzweig and Schultz (1982, 1983, 1988), and Grossman and Joyce (1990)). There are unexplained racial and ethnic patterns in birthweight that parallel the IMR differentials described above. Birthweight appears to have been less affected by technological change over time than the IMR — it seems that in the United States, technology has been used more successfully to save low birthweight babies than to improve birth outcomes.

iii) Anthropometrics and Nutritional Status

Height-for-age and weight-for-height are anthropometric measures of the

TABLE 3

Percent of Children Less than the NCHS Fifth Percentile of Height for Age and Weight for Height by Age, Sex and Poverty Status, 1976-1980

	Females		Males	
	Poverty	Nonpoverty	Poverty	Nonpoverty
Height for Age				
2-5 Years	14.7%	5.3%	11.1%	5.3%
6-11 Years	6.8	4.0	6.8	3.6
12-17 Years	7.3	2.7	7.5	4.4
Weight for Height				
2-5 Years	3.3	2.5	2.1	2.4
6-9 Years	1.1	2.4	6.9	2.3

Source: National Health and Nutrition Examination Survey II, 1976-80.

health and nutritional status of older children that have been used success-fully in the Development Economics and Economic History literatures (see for example, Fogel (1986), Martorell and Habicht (1986), Thomas (1991), Floud *et al.* (1990)). The evidence suggests that well-nourished children in many societies follow similar growth curves and it has been argued that height, conditional on age and gender, is a good indicator of longer run nutritional and health status, while weight, conditional on height and gen-der is a good shorter run measure. Weight-for-height is sometimes used and interpreted as an intermediate measure, with malnourishment reflected in both highly over and under-weight children.

Growth varies systematically with age and gender so heights and weights are usually standardized using guidelines from the National Center for Health Statistics (1976). Each child in a sample is compared with the median child in a population of well nourished children of the same age and gender in the United States; each child's height-for-age and weight-for-height are expressed as a percentage of these medians.

Table 3 indicates that the incidence of stunting (low height-for-age) and wasting (low weight-for-height) is much greater among poor than among non-poor children. A 1983 study carried out by the Massachusetts Depart-ment of Health found that 9.8% of poor preschool children in Massachu-setts had a height-for-age below the 5th percentile of the NCHS standards (Massachusetts Department of Health, 1983). Hence these anthropometric measures appear to be useful indicators of child nutritional status even in as rich a country as the United States where actual starvation is uncommon.

The NCHS norms are not perfect and care must be exercised when com-paring children of different ages or races. The growth curves of poor chil-dren in many countries show systematic deviations from the growth curves of the median child (Waterlow, *et al.*, 1977). Figure 2 illustrates a typical pattern using data from the National Longitudinal Survey's Child-Mother file (NLSCM), which over-samples poor children in the United States. The figure shows that among these children, growth tends to falter in infancy but catches up to the median US child after age 2. It is also true that in spite of the fact that the NLSCM is a sample of relatively poor children, the height of the average child (conditional on age and gender) is only slightly below the US median. This is partly because African-Americans are significantly taller than whites and the NLSCM over-sampled African-Americans. These facts suggest that it is important to compare children of the same race who are of approximately similar ages.

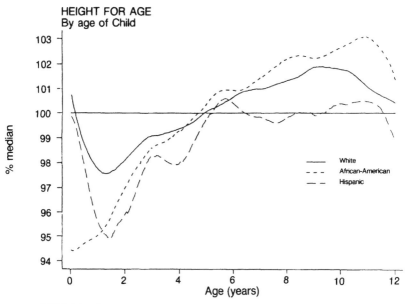

FIGURE 2   Non parametric estimates

Another potential problem is that reported heights and weights are not always accurately measured. In the NLSCM, child heights and weights are either measured (by the enumerator or mother) or recalled by the mother. The probability of being measured rises with age, while the variance of normalized heights and weights declines. This pattern suggests that the measured data are less subject to error than the maternal reports, and that the heights and weights of very young children are likely to be most affected by measurement error.

Finally, it is clear that there is a genetic component to a child's height and weight. Hence, it is important to control for parental height and weight, if possible. On the other hand, height and weight are not entirely genetically determined. Evidence of environmental effects comes from studies that have followed uniform groups over time. For example, in Britain in 1883, the difference in mean height between the upper and lower classes was more than 8 inches. By 1961, the difference had shrunk to between 1.5 and 2 inches (Birch and Gussow, 1970).[9]

---

[9] For more evidence on this question see Birch and Gussow (1970), Chapter 5.

A more direct way to assess nutritional status is to use information about the nutrients 'available' in the household's usual diet and information from biochemical tests. Data about usual diets is collected by means of asking respondents to recall their food expenditures and/or food intakes, or by having them keep diaries that record food expenditures and/or intakes over some period of time. Nutrient availability will generally exceed nutrient intake because of wastage, food given to guests, pets, and so on.

Nutrient intakes are usually measured as a proportion of the US Recommended Daily Allowance (RDA). RDAs vary with age and gender and are set to provide sufficient nutrients for virtually every health person in a given group. Hence, they will tend to over-state the nutritional requirements of the average person.

Measures of nutrient availability and intakes typically focus on a short recent period such as the last 24 hours, or the last week. Since the body can compensate for many short-term dietary inadequacies, it is useful to have a measure of the level of nutrients in the body. Biochemical tests of blood and urine can be used for this purpose. Data from the National Health and Nutrition Examination Survey II, show that low-income children are more likely to suffer from iron and zinc deficiencies. For example, 20.6% of 1-to 2-year-old children in low-income households suffer iron anemia compared to 6.7% of 1- to 2-year-olds from higher income households (Devaney, Haines, and Moffitt, 1989).

These deficiencies have been linked to growth retardation, lethargy, impaired immune status, and slow healing of wounds. Even mild cases of iron deficiency anemia can have serious consequences on a child's ability to learn: anemic children have shorter attention spans, poor concentration, increased fatigue, and increased irritability (Parker, 1989).

iv) Illnesses

Another way to assess health status is to ask how often a child is seriously ill. A prototypical question might ask 'How many times was the child taken to see a doctor for illness in the last year?' By asking only about illnesses that resulted in a doctor's visit, the question seeks to screen out trivial illnesses. It is also possible that illnesses that did not result in a doctor's visit are less likely to be remembered, and therefore that including them would make the data more sensitive to recall errors.

Unfortunately, the number of doctor's visits is likely to depend on many factors other than the frequency and severity of illness. In fact, the number of doctor visits tends to rise with income and with the education of the

TABLE 4
Relative Frquency of Health Problems
in Low-income Children Compared with Other Children

Health problem	Relative frequency in low-income children
Asthma	higher
Bacterial meningitis	double
Rheumatic fever	double-triple
Lead poisoning	triple
Complications of appendicitis	double-triple
Diabetic ketoacidosis	double
Complications of bacterial meningitis	double-triple
Percent with conditions limiting School activity	double-triple
Child deaths due to accidents	double-triple
Child deaths due to disease	triple-quadruple
Lost school days	40% more
Severely impaired vision	double-triple
Severe iron-deficiency anemia	double

Source: Starfield (1985).

mother, even though health generally improves with socio-economic status (Feinstein (1992), Black (1988)). The child's health insurance coverage, access to medical care, race, and the parents' attitudes towards doctors and illness all play a part in determining the number of visits. The number of visits also tends to decline with age.

With regard to the role of health insurance, the RAND Health Insurance Experiment (a social experiment that randomly assigned subjects to a variety of health insurance treatments) has shown that the number of out-patient pediatric visits rises with the generosity of health insurance coverage. On the other hand, pediatiric in-patient hospital visits are not significantly affected by insurance coverage (Leibowitz, 1985). These results suggest that in-patient visits may be a cleaner measure of health status than either the number of out-patient visits or the total number of visits.[10] However, since relatively few children are hospitalized, reliance on this measure may lead to small sample sizes. Another caveat is that there are substantial geo-

[10] The RAND Insurance Experiment also cast some doubt on the link between utilization of medical care and health since they did not detect any measurable relationship between the two. On the other hand, their sample of children was quite small, and 6 out of 8 clinical measures of health status showed positive but insignificant effects of increased utilization. Clearly, the issue requires further study.

graphic variations in pediatric hospitalization rates which suggest that they reflect differences in practice style as well as morbidity (Homer, 1988).

Differential access to care, or differing attitudes towards doctors and illness could explain persistent racial differentials in the number of pediatric visits for illness. African-American and white children have very different 'visit rates'. In 1989, visit rates were 108 per 1000 children under 21 for whites and 77 per 1000 for African-Americans (Woodwell, 1989). Reis (1990) reports that African-American children have fewer doctor visits than white children at all income level. The Centers for Disease Control reports that even among children with chronic health conditions, African-American children have fewer doctor visits although they are more likely to be hospitalized (Aday, 1992).

It is true however, that poor children are at greater risk than richer ones for a variety of specific illnesses, as shown in Table 4. This suggests that a focus on specific conditions may be more useful in assessing health status than counting the number of visits.

Finally, it is interesting to note the interaction between illness and nutritional status. Just as poor nutrition can lead to impaired immune status, serious illness can lead to deficits in levels of protein, vitamin A, and vitamin C in the body (Birch and Gussow, 1970).

v) Preventive Care

Measures of the utilization of preventive care break the link between medical attention and illness, and measure only access and attitudes towards care. The measures of preventive care that are most frequently available are whether the child has had a recent checkup (or a 'well visit') and whether the child has had recommended immunizations. In 1985, 30 to 40% of white children and 50 to 60% of 'all other' children had not been immunized against the common childhood diseases (US House of Representatives, 1992).

The recommended schedule of preventive pediatric care depends on the child's age — in general, the older the child, the less frequently he or she needs to have a checkup. Standard medical practice also changes over time. Homer (1988) notes a trend in recommendations from the American Academy of Pediatrics towards increasing numbers of visits over the past 15 years.

According to Homer, the Academy 'forthrightly admits the arbitrary nature of its schedule'. The arbitrariness is due to the paucity of evidence regarding the efficacy of well-child care. For example, a Canadian task force charged with making recommendations to provincial health ministers about periodic health examinations found that dental examinations and immunizations were the only interventions for which evidence of efficacy existed.

In his survey of the literature, Homer concludes that child health supervision 'as now performed' has little effect on childhood mortality or morbidity. On the other hand, he notes that the sample sizes used may have been too small to adequately identify changes and that in many cases the measures of morbidity used have been 'poorly suited to the pediatric population'. Moreover, there is some evidence that well-child care can reduce the frequency of hospitalization for acute illness.

Prenatal care is another important type of preventive care. Prenatal care that is adequate in terms of timeliness and the number of visits has been shown to significantly reduce the risk of low birth weight and infant mortality (Institute of Medicine, 1985). The infant mortality rates for white and Afican-American women with no visits are 31.2 and 56.5 per 1000, respectively, while women with 13 to 16 visits have infant mortality rates of 4.1 if white and 7.4 if African-American (Eberstadt, 1991). Despite this link between prenatal care and improved birth outcomes, 22% of white women and 41% of African-American women delayed obtaining prenatal care until the second trimester of pregnancy in 1989. Poor women and teenagers were the least likely to obtain timely care (National Center for Health Statistics, 1991).

vi) Activity Limitations

'Activity limitations' are among the most common measures of health status. Typically parents are asked how many days a child had to spend in bed, or how many days a child missed school over some period of time. These measures are subject to the same problems as the number of doctor visits for illness.

B. Test Scores and Scholastic Achievement

Academic achievement is a very important determinant of a child's success in our society: Each additional year of high school is estimated to raise future wages by as much as 8% (cf. Welch, 1973) and improvements in education are responsible for much of the narrowing of the wage gap between whites and African-Americans that has occurred over this century (Smith and Welch, 1989). It is not surprising then, that many tests of academic potential and achievement have been developed. These tests are controversial: typically, African-Americans obtain poorer scores than whites, and depending on the test, girls may outperform boys or vice-versa. And it is not clear that these tests are ultimately good predictors of academic success, once measures of a child's background are adequately controlled for. Indeed, many would argue that test scores provide a better measure of background than of true academic potential.

Test scores may also be biased by the child's degree of rapport with the interviewer. For example, in the NLSCM, the correlation between the interviewer's assessment of the child's degree of sociability and other test scores is generally positive and significant (Baker and Mott, 1989). And Zigler *et al.*, (1973) suggests that disadvantaged children may attain lower scores due to a greater degree of test anxiety.

Many widely used tests have 'norms' that have been calibrated using nationally representative samples. In principle, these norms can help to determine the representativeness of a given sample of children. However, some tests such as the Peabody Individual Achievement Tests (PIATS) were normed as long ago as the 1960s. Since rudimentary mathematics and reading skills appear to have improved over time in the general population, the use of old norms can produce surprising results. For example, Baker and Mott (1989) note that in the NLSCM, the average child scored 105 on the PIAT Mathematics test, whereas the norming sample had a mean of 100. Scores are often normed by age or by gender. However, as discussed above for the case of the anthropometric measures, norms are imperfect and it is advisable to compare children within relatively narrow age bands and to check for gender differences.

Most tests focus on particular aspects of academic achievement. Examples are the Peabody Picture Vocabulary Test (PPVT), the PIAT Reading Comprehension Test, and the PIAT Mathematics Test. It is unwise to make too much of achievement on a single test because it does not measure all aspects of achievement, and achievement on a single test is not always highly correlated with achievement on other tests. For example, in the NLSCM, the correlation between the PPVT and the PIAT Mathematics test scores is only .26 among 6 year olds (Baker and Mott, 1989).

More direct measures of academic attainment are whether a child has ever taken remedial courses or been retained in grade. There is a great deal of evidence that suggests that children who lag behind their peers at early ages are at higher risk of dropping out of high school later on (cf. Ensminger and Slusarcick, 1992).

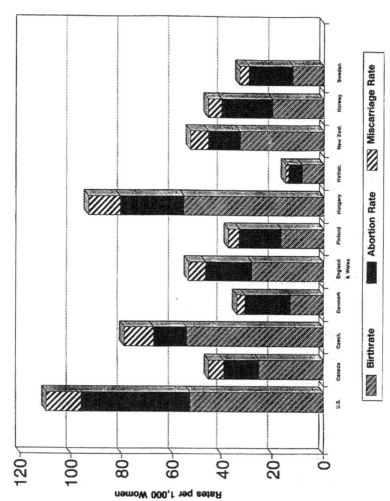

FIGURE 3   Birth rate, abortion rate, and pregnancy rate per 1,000 women aged 15–19, 11 countries, 1983.

C. Long-Run Measures of Social Competency

The War on Poverty was launched in the hope of 'breaking the cycle of poverty' – a goal that can only be said to have been reached if welfare programs prevent poor children from becoming poor adults. Hence, one measure of the success of welfare programs is the long-run situation of the children whose parents participated. Are they less likely to become pregnant as teenager, to engage in delinquency and crime, to be out of the labor force, or ultimately to have their own children participate in welfare programs?

The remainder of this section briefly outlines the dimensions of the teen pregnancy, high school drop-out, non-employment, and juvenile crime problems. Clearly, any program that reduced their incidence at reasonable cost could be judged a success. However, very little work has been done examining long-range outcomes of this kind because it is so difficult to sort out the effects of parental welfare participation from the effects of family background and community characteristics.

Figure 3 shows that relative to many countries, the US has a very high rate of teen pregnancy. One recent study estimates that the government spends $22 billion per year to provide AFDC, Food Stamps, and Medicaid coverage to families started by teen mothers (Center for Population Options, 1990). In addition, teen pregnancy can be extremely costly to both mother and child. Forty percent of teenage girls who drop out of school do so because of pregnancy or marriage, and teen mothers are twice as likely to be poor as other mothers (Edelman, 1987). Finally, teen mothers are more likely to delay prenatal care and are at higher risk of bearing low birthweight babies than other mothers.

Children of adolescent mothers continue to be disadvantaged in latter life. They are less likely to complete high school and have lower earnings as adults, have higher rates of delinquency, and are more likely to ultimately become single parents themselves (McLanahan *et al.*, 1991). Whether these disadvantages reflect the effects of growing up in a single-parent family itself or other factors like the poverty often associated with living in a female-headed household is hotly debated. The question is taken up in Chapter 4.

Although rates of high school non-completion have fallen over time, in 1990 14% of persons 25 to 29 years old reported that they had not completed high school (US Bureau of the Census, 1991). The rate is highest among African-Americans at 25%. There are also racial disparities in rates of college completion. Twenty-three percent of whites 25 to 29 years old had completed at least 4 years of college compared to only 13% of African-Americans (US Bureau of the Census, 1992).

People without at least a high school education face great difficulties in the labor market that are reflected in high rates of unemployment and non-employment (i.e. withdrawal from the labor market). In 1986, 12% of white male high school dropouts and 40% of African-American male high school dropouts 20 to 24 years old reported that they had gained no work experience at all in the previous year (Markey, 1988).

This lack of labor market attachment is sometimes linked to high crime rates among young men. On any given day in 1987, 53,500 juveniles were in custody in public correctional facilities. During the course of the year, over half a million juveniles were admitted to these facilities. These youthful offenders were disproportionately male and African-American. Most were 14 to 17 years old. Ninety-four percent were being held for offenses that would have been criminal had they been charged as adults (US House Select Committee on Children, Youth and Families, 1989).

D. Other Measures

The largest residual category of measures are psycho-social measures of a child's home environment, development, self-esteem, and relationships with others. Using parental reports from the National Health Interview Survey of Child Health, Zill and Schoeborn (1990) report that 4% of US children suffer some type of developmental delay and 6.5% have had an emotional or behavioral problem that lasted 3 months or more or required psychological treatment. Only half of the 10.7 million children whose parents reported some type of developmental or emotional disorders had received any treatment. This monograph will focus on more quantitative measures of child well-being, not because psycho-social measures are unimportant but because the author has no expertise in assessing them and it is necessary to limit the scope of the survey.

3. THE PROGRAMS

Virtually any social welfare program affects children to the extent that it has direct or indirect effects on the family. This monograph focuses on federal programs that are directly targeted to families with children. Block grants from the federal government to states for social services and compensatory education, as well as state programs such as general assistance are excluded in order to keep the number of programs manageable.[11] This chapter provides a brief discussion of the major programs as they exist today, an analysis of trends in caseloads and expenditures, a comparison of government expenditures on children with expenditures on the elderly, and a discussion of the anti-poverty effectiveness of the programs.

A. An Overview of Spending on Programs that Benefit Children.[12]

Table 5 describes federal spending in 1990 for programs targeted to children. These estimates exclude administrative costs whenever possible and also exclude state matching contributions for Aid to Families with Dependent Children (AFDC) and Medicaid. Since some of these programs also benefit families without children, each line shows both total spending on the program, and an estimate of the percent of spending that goes directly to families with children.

The table shows that the three largest programs in terms of expenditures on children are AFDC, Food Stamps, and Medicaid. Other large programs include housing assistance, the National School Lunch Program, the Special Supplemental Feeding Program for Women, Infants, and Children (WIC), and Head Start. Tax expenditures are not usually thought of as 'welfare', but Table 5 indicates that transfers in the form of tax credits make up a large part of the total support provided to poor families with children.

i) AFDC

AFDC is the largest cash transfer program. It was originally authorized

---

[11] Another reason for excluding block grants and state programs is that information about these programs is not available from any central source. Federal programs that benefit handicapped children and other federal educational programs are excluded on the grounds that they are not 'welfare programs.' In 1990, block grants for compensatory education, programs for the handicapped, and other educational programs cost $8.2 billion.

[12] Unless otherwise noted, the information in this chapter comes from the US House of Representatives (1991, 1992).

TABLE 5
Federal Spending in Fiscal Year 1990
for Programs Targeted to Children (billions of dollars)[1]

Program	Total[2]	Percent Spent on Children
Cash transfers:		
AFDC	10.1	100
In-kind transfers:		
Food Stamps	15.1	81
WIC	2.1	100
School Lunch and Other Child Nutrition[3]	5.5	100
Medicaid	41.1	29
Housing Assistance[4]	15.3	49
Education:		
Head Start	1.6	100
Other Services:[5]	5.0	87
Subtotal:	95.8	59
Tax Credits:		
Earned Income Tax Credit		
Outlay	5.3	86
Revenue Loss	1.6	89
Dependent Care Credit	2.6	95
Subtotal:	9.5	90
Total:	105.3	62

Notes:

1. This table is adapted from the one in US House of Representatives (1991), page 1345. Column 2 excludes 22 billion dollars in payments to families with children from Social Security, Supplemental Security, Unemployment Insurance, the Low Income Home Energy Assistance Program, and Veteran's Compensation. See Table 9 for total expenditures on AFDC and Medicaid including state spending.

2. See Table 9, footnote 1.

3. Includes school breakfasts and lunches, special meal assistance, summer and child care feeding, and special milk programs. About 3.7 billion is for the National School Lunch program.

4. Housing assistance includes public and Indian housing, rent supplements, and housing projects provided under Sections 8, 235, and 236.

5. Includes child support enforcement, foster care and adoption assistance, maternal and child health programs, summer youth employment and training, child abuse and family violence spending, programs for runaway and homeless youth, Title III services, services for children with developmental disabilities, Work Incentives/JOBS programs, imunizations, and the Juvenile Justice Program.

under the Social Security Act of 1935, as a federal-state matching entitlement that would provide assistance to fatherless children. The fact that it is an entitlement means that anyone who meets the eligibility criteria can receive benefits. AFDC is administered at the state level within federal guidelines –states choose the need and payment standards that determine eligibility[13], set income and asset limits, and choose benefit levels. As a result, program characteristics vary considerably from state to state. For example, as of January 1991, the maximum AFDC grant for a one-parent family of 4 persons varied from $124 a month in Alabama to $891 in Alaska. The federal poverty line for a family of 4 persons was $13,942 per year. On average the federal government pays 54% of benefit costs, and 50% of administrative costs.

As of October 1, 1990, all states are also required to offer an AFDC Unemployed Parent (AFDC-UP) program to two-parent families in which one of the parents is unemployed. Some states have offered this program since 1961, when the federal government first authorized it. Eligibility for AFDC-UP is restricted to families in which the principal wage earner has strong labor force attachments. As a result, only 5% of AFDC families qualified under this program in 1990.[14]

The average AFDC household has 3 persons, including 1 or 2 AFDC recipients. In 41% of AFDC households, the youngest child is under 3 years old. Fifty-four percent of the children are eligible because their mother is single, while a further 33% became eligible as a result of divorce or separation. Twenty-three percent of the mothers have less than a 12th grade education, compared to 12% of all adult women. Thirty-eight percent of AFDC mothers are white, 40% are African-American, and 17% are Hispanic. Currently, about 60% of children in poverty are served by the AFDC program.

Most 'spells' of AFDC receipt are relatively short: once multiple spells are accounted for, 30% of AFDC spells last less than 2 years and 50% last less than 4 years (Ellwood and Bane, cited in Commitee on Ways and Means, 1992). On the other hand, at any point in time 65% of the caseload is made up of people who are in the midst of spells of 8 years or more. Hence, the lion's share of resources are spent on long-term recipients.

Most research has focused on the fact that people on AFDC have little monetary incentive to work. After 'disregards' for $30 of earned income, a standard household deduction, 'excess shelter costs', child care expenses,

---

[13] To qualify for AFDC, a family must have a gross income less than 185% of the state need standard and must have a countable income less than the state's payment standard. In 29 states, the payment standard is below the need standard.

[14] The number is projected to rise to 7% by 1995.

work expenses, and the Earned Income Tax Credit (if received), benefits are reduced a dollar for each dollar a women earns, and for each dollar received in child support. See the discussion of Table 7 below for an illustration of the way that these disregards are implemented.

The high implicit tax rate may discourage eligible women with other income sources from using the program: Blank and Ruggles (1993) find that only half of eligible women use AFDC. High tax rates also seem to be a significant disincentive to market work: only 7% of AFDC mothers report that they work, and only 20% report any non-AFDC cash income. However in a study of 50 AFDC mothers in Chicago, Edin (1991) found that half of the mothers supplemented their AFDC income with earned income. Seven mothers actually worked full-time at regular low-wage jobs while 22 mothers worked part-time or at odd jobs. These numbers suggest that the extent to which AFDC mothers are cut off from the mainstream labor market has been exaggerated in studies using survey data.

ii) The Food Stamp Program

The Food Stamp Program grew out of efforts to transfer surplus agricultural commodities to the needy during the Great Depression. These programs were formalized and extended to all states in the Food Stamp Act of 1964. Changes to the program in 1971 and 1973 established uniform eligibility requirements and established the program in all counties in the United States (Clarkson, 1975).[15]

Food Stamps are issued in the form of booklets of coupons which may be used to purchase all foods excluding alcohol, tobacco, and hot foods 'intended for immediate consumption'. In contrast to AFDC, Food Stamps are available to all families who meet federally determined income-eligibility requirements, though AFDC recipients are automatically eligible. Food Stamp income is reduced by $.30 for every dollar of countable income (including AFDC benefits), once certain disregards are applied.

iii) Medicaid and Child Health

Medicaid is the single most important health insurance program for poor children, accounting for over 55% of public expenditures on child health. It was created in 1966 as a federal-state matching entitlement with the stated goal of eliminating financial barriers to medical care. In 1967, the program

---

[15] The Food Stamp Act of 1977 also eliminated a requirement that better-off eligible households purchase a portion of their Food Stamp allotments.

was amended to include Early and Periodic Screening Diagnosis and Treatment (EPSDT) services.

The Medicaid program provides health insurance to eligible poor families and to the aged, blind, and disabled. Table 5 shows that the lion's share of the expenditures are accounted for by the aged, blind, and disabled. The average annual expenditure on a AFDC child is $682 compared to $5928 for an aged person and $1290 for an AFDC adult (US House of Representatives, 1991). States are required to offer Medicaid coverage to AFDC recipients and to AFDC-UP families and, until recently, there was a very close linkage between AFDC recipiency and Medicaid eligibility.[16]

EPSDT was designed to provide comprehensive screening services to children under 21 as well as treatment for problems discovered during screening. Until recently, states were allowed to establish the number of screenings they would cover and the age intervals when children would receive them. States were only required to cover treatment services that were mandatory for all Medicaid-eligible persons, and were allowed to impose restrictions on the eligibility of providers. Federal data shows that only 39% of eligible children participate in EPSDT. Participation rates range from as low as 7% in Delaware and Oklahoma to as high as 96% in Arizona (US DHHS, July 1990).

In an effort to address the high rates of infant mortality and low birthweight discussed in Chapter 2, Congress began extending Medicaid coverage for pregnant women and children in 1984. The laws extending Medicaid coverage are outlined in Table 6. States are now required to cover all pregnant women and children under 6 with family income less than 133% of the federal poverty line, regardless of family structure[17] As of July 1, 1991, states were also required to cover all children born after September 30, 1983 whose family incomes were less than 100% of the federal poverty line. States are also permitted to extend Medicaid coverage to groups of 'medically needy' people with incomes less than a standard determined by the state.[18] Forty-one states now have a Medically Needy program. However at $2.9 billion, payments to mothers and children under the Medically Needy pro-

---

[16] States are also required to extend coverage to people who go off AFDC for 4 to 12 months, depending on the reason for the loss of coverage.

[17] The federal poverty line does not vary from state to state. The coverage of pregnant women is limited to services related to the pregnancy.

[18] This standard cannot exceed 133.33% of the state's maximum AFDC payment for a similar family. The Medically Needy are those whose incomes have been reduced below this standard by large medical expenditures.

TABLE 6
Major Federal Expansions of Medicaid
Relating to Children, 1984-1990

Law	Eligibility expansions
Deficit Reduction Act of 1984	Requires coverage of all children born after 9/30/83 meeting State AFDC income and resource standards, regardless of family structure. Requires automatic coverage for 1 year after birth if mother already is receiving Medicaid and remains eligible, and infant resides with her.
Consolidated Omnibus Budget Reconcilitation Act (COBRA) of 1985	Allows extension of DEFRA coverage up to age 5 immediately, instead of requiring a phase-in by birth date. Requires coverage of adoptive and foster children even if adoption/foster agreement was entered into in another State. Requires coverage of children with special needs regardless of income/resources of adoptive/foster parents. Extended 60 days of postpartum coverage to women who were on Medicaid while pregnant, making the unborn child what determines the size of assistance unit.
Omnibus Budget Reconciliation Act (OBRA) of 1986	Creates new optional categorically needy group for pregnant women and infants (children up to age 1) with incomes below 100% of the poverty line and allows assets test to be dropped for this group. Allows phased coverage of children up to age 5 if incomes are below 100% of the poverty line. Requires continuation of elgibility (for those who otherwise would become ineligible) if they are hospital inpatients when the age limits is reached. Allows states to waive assets tests and adopt presumptive eligibility for pregnant women.
Omnibus Budget Reconciliation Act (OBRA) of 1987	Allows coverage of pregnant women and infants (children up to age 1) with incomes below 185% of the poverty line. Allows immediate extension of OBRA-86 coverage of children up to age 5 with incomes below 100% of the poverty line. Allows coverage for children aged 5-7 with incomes up to the State AFDC level (phased in by age). Allows coverage for children below age 9 with incomes up to 100% of poverty line (phased in by age).
Medicare Catastrophic Coverage Act (MCCA) of 1988	Makes mandatory the OBRA-86 option of coverage of pregnant women and infants (children up to age 1) with incomes up to 100% of the poverty line (phased in by % of poverty line). Allows States to use more liberal criteria than that used for the AFDC program to determine Medicaid financial eligibility.

TABLE 6 (Continued)

Law	Eligibility expansions
Family Support Act of 1988	Increases required period of Medicaid coverage for families whose AFDC cash assistance is lost due to earnings. Required coverage of AFDC families with an unemployed parent.
Omnibus Budget Reconciliation Act (OBRA) of 1989	Requires coverage of pregnant women and infants (children up to age 1) with incomes below 133% of the poverty line. Requires coverage of children up to age 6 with incomes below 133% of the poverty line.
Omnibus Budget Reconciliation Act (OBRA) of 1990	Requires coverage of children up to age 19 with income below 100% of the poverty line (phased in by age). Requires States to receive and process applications at convenient outreach sites. Requires continuous eligibility of children up to age 1, who were born to Medicaid-eligible mothers and remain in mother's household.

gram amounted to only a fraction of the expenditures made under the Medicaid program.

States are required by the federal government to offer certain services such as preventive pediatric care for children under the Medicaid program. Other services such as drugs and eyeglasses are optional. However, states may limit the amount of care provided within a service category. For example, some states have limits on the length of hospital visits. States also determine how the program will be administered and set reimbursement policies for doctors and hospitals. As a result, the coverage provided by Medicaid varies substantially from state to state.

iv) Housing Assistance

Housing assistance has been provided since 1937 under the auspices of the Department of Housing and Urban Development (HUD). In contrast to AFDC, Food Stamps, and Medicaid, housing assistance is not an entitlement: when funds allocated to the program run out, people who are eligible for the program must be wait-listed. As Table 5 indicates, it is estimated that about half of federal expenditures on housing assistance directly benefit children. The elderly are the other large group of beneficiaries.

The major forms in which rental assistance is offered are: 1) low-rent public housing, 2) Section 8 new construction/substantial rehabilitation, and 3) Section 8 existing housing. The federal government also offers mortgage assistance to low-income rural households. Low-rent public housing is what most people think of as 'public housing'. In the past, local housing authorities built low-rent units. Today, they are permitted to lease existing structures and to purchase privately developed ('turnkey') units.

The Section 8 programs were established by the Housing and Community Development Act of 1974. Under the new construction/rehabilitation part of the program, the federal government subsidizes the rents of apartments brought into the stock by private developers. Contracts between the developers and HUD are for 5 years, renewable for 20 to 40 years depending on the type of financing. Many section 8 contracts are due to expire in the 1990s which means that it will require substantial appropriations just to maintain the low-income housing stock at existing levels (Lazere et al., 1991).

The Section 8 existing housing programs provides rent subsidies to families who find an apartment of their own choosing, as long as the rent is below the 'Fair Market Rent' established by HUD, and the unit meets minimum quality standards. Rental assistance typically reduces a family's rental payments to 30% of its income, after deductions for certain expenses are taken into account. The Congressional Budget Office estimates that since 1982, over two-thirds of new authorizations for rental housing assistance were for Section 8 programs (Pedone, 1988).

It is important to note that, as shown in Figure 4, direct spending on housing assistance for the poor is small in comparison to federal 'tax expenditures' on housing. Deductions for mortgage interest and property taxes cost the federal government an estimated $78.4 billion in 1990 (Lazere et al., 1991). Poterba (1992) estimates that more than half of the tax savings from the mortgage interest deduction accrued to the top 8.5% of tax returns in 1988. In part, this is because few low-income households itemize.

v) School Lunch, WIC, and Other Child Nutrition Programs[19]

The federal government supports 7 programs that provide meals or monthly food supplements to low-income children. The largest are the National School Lunch Program (NSLP), the School Breakfast Program (SBP) and the Special Supplemental Feeding Program for Women, Infants, and Children (WIC). The meal programs are entitlements that operate by reimbursing schools for each meal served. In additiion, these programs provide commodity assistance to schools and residential institutions that serve meals to children. In 1981, the NSLP served as the outlet for 98% of the surplus food donated by

---

[19] Some of the information in this section is taken from Jones (1990, 1992).

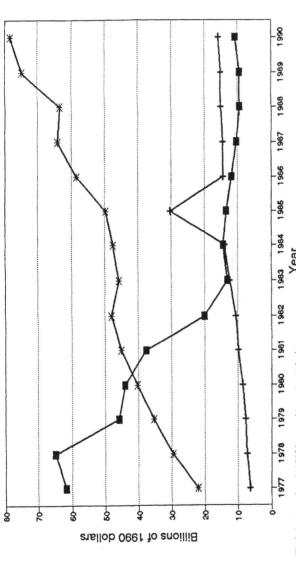

Note: The bulge in outlays in 1985 is caused by a change in the method of financing public housing, which generated close to $14 billion in one-time expenditures. This amount paid off–all at once–the capital cost of public housing construction and modernization activities undertaken between 1974 and 1985, which otherwise would have been paid off over periods of up to 40 years. Because of this one-time expenditure, however, future outlays for public housing will be lower than they would have been otherwise.

FIGURE 4 Federal housing expenditures

the federal government to all sources (Radzikowski and Gale, 1984). The WIC program is funded by appropriations and the size of each year's appropriation limits the number of people that can be served.

The NSLP was begun in 1946 in response to national concern about the fact that one-third of World War II draftees were unfit for service because of deficiencies thought to be nutrition-related. It is by far the largest of the child nutrition program: In 1981, lunches were served to approximately 25 million students in 98% of the public schools – enough to feed 60% of all students attending public schools (Radzikowski and Gale, 1984a, b). School lunches are provided free to children with family incomes less than 130% of the federal poverty line, and are subsidized if the family income falls between 130 and 185% of the poverty line. Forty percent of these lunches were provided free to low income children.

The School Breakfast Program was instituted in 1966. It serves far fewer children than the lunch program: In 1981, about 4 million breakfasts were served in 33,000 schools, enough to feed about 10% of the public school student body.[20] This difference in size is reflected in the relative cost of the programs: in 1990, the SBP cost $600 million compared to $3.8 billion for the NSLP. Participants in the SBP tend to be poorer than participants in the NSLP – 80% of school breakfasts were served free.

The WIC program provides nutritional counseling and food supplements to pregnant and lactating mothers and their infants as well as to low-income children up to age 5. It is currently operated out of some 8,330 sites. The law requires that WIC provide foods containing protein, iron, calcium, vitamin A, and vitamin C.

Food packages must be appropriately tailored to meet the needs of each category of recipient.[21] In fiscal year 1991, the average monthly WIC package was valued at $31.67.

WIC participants must have family incomes less than 185% of the poverty line, (though states may set income thresholds as low as 100% of the poverty line) and must be nutritionally at risk. To be certified 'at risk', a participant must have a documented nutritionally-related medical condition, a health-impairing dietary deficiency, or a condition that predisposes people to inadequate nutrition or to medical problems. Evaluation of WIC

---

[20] These numbers have remained relatively constant over time.

[21] The categories are children 0 to 3 months of age, 4 to 12 months, women and children with special dietary needs, children from 1 to 5, pregnant and nursing mothers, and postpartum non-nursing mothers.

is complicated by the fact that providers do not use uniform criteria for certifying nutritional risk. Participants must be re-certified at intervals in order to continue in the program. WIC currently serves an estimated 60% of those eligible. According to the Congressional Budget Office, it would have cost $3.75 billion, or 44% more than that year's appropriation, to serve all those who were eligible in 1992.

vi) Head Start

Head Start is a federal matching grant program that aims to improve the learning skills, social skills, and health status of poor children so that they can begin schooling on an equal footing with their more advantaged peers. Federal guidelines require that 90% of the children served be from families with incomes below the federal poverty line. Given that there are over 1,300 Head Start programs (Hayes, *et al.*, 1990), all administered at a local level, and that the program guidelines are not specific about how the goals of the program are to be attained, there is a great deal of variation in program content.

Begun in 1964 as part of President Johnson's 'War on Poverty', Head Start is one element of that program that has enjoyed great public and bi-partisan support. Former President Bush and President Clinton have both pledged to increase federal funding so that all eligible children may be served. In 1992, 622,000 children, roughly 28% of eligible 3-to 5-year-olds, were served at a cost of $2.2 billion (Stewart, 1992).

vii) Tax Credits [22]

The earned income tax credit (EITC) was introduced in 1975 as a means of granting tax relief to low-income families. In 1992, the maximum EITC was $1,324 for tax payers with one qualifying child and $1,384 for tax pay-ers with additional qualifying children. The EITC begins to be phased out for tax payers with adjusted gross income (AGI) above $11,840 and was completely phased out for tax payers with AGI greater than $22,370. Scholz (1993) estimates that in 1990, between 80 and 86% of eligible tax payers received the EITC.

The Omnibus Reconciliation Act of 1993 (OBRA '93) will lead to a major expansion of this credit. By 1998, when it is fully in place, federal spending on the EITC will be one and a half times as large as federal spending on

---

[22] The information in this section is drawn from Eissa and Leibman (1994), Scholz (1993), and US House of Representatives (1991, 1992).

AFDC. When the changes are fully implemented, it is estimated that 6 million families below the poverty line will receive credits, and 1 million families will be raised out of poverty by them. However, half of the payments made under the program will be to families with incomes above the poverty line. The EITC will also be made available to poor families without children for the first time.

Unlike most tax credits, the EITC is 'refundable', that is, if the amount of the credit exceeds the tax payer's federal income tax liability then the difference is refunded. Table 5 shows that in fact most EITC were outlays of this kind rather than foregone tax dollars. EITC recipients are older, better educated, have fewer children, and are more likely to be white than AFDC recipients. Most work long hours at low wages.

Eissa and Liebman (1994) find that the dynamics of EITC recipiency are similar to those of AFDC recipiency: while less than a third of EITC recipients are still receiving the credit two years later, about half of them claim the credit at least three more times in the next nine years. However, in contrast to AFDC, EITC recipients are more likely to 'exit' the program by way of working than by way of marriage: during the 1980s, former recipients stopped qualifying for the following reasons – a third raised their earnings above the threshold; 10% no longer had a dependent child; 10 to 15% raised their income by marrying; and 5 to 10% no longer had an earned income.

The Dependent Care Tax Credit allows families with two earners to deduct up to 30% of employment-related dependent care expenses. In 1992, the credit was capped at $2,400 for one child and $4,800 for two or more children. Unlike the EITC, it is not refundable. Since the lion's share of the credit is claimed by families who are not in poverty, it is not considered a 'welfare' program for the purposes of this monograph.

viii) Interactions Between the Programs

The discussion above makes it clear that many children are covered by more than one program. As discussed above, AFDC participants are covered by Medicaid and are automatically eligible for Food Stamps. As of 1990, half of AFDC children received free school lunches, 35% lived in public or subsidized rental housing, and 19% participated in WIC. Conversely, half of all Food Stamp recipients, 42% of Medicaid recipients, 38% of WIC recipients, and 24% of those in public housing also received AFDC. Moffitt (1992) estimates that in 1984, 26.4% of non-elderly single-parent families received AFDC, Medicaid, and Food Stamps, and 11% received at least one benefit in addition to AFDC.

TABLE 7
Earnings and Benefits for a Mother with Two Children with Daycare Expenses
After 4 Months on Job (January 1991) – (Pennsylvania)

Earnings	EITC[1]	EITC[2]	Food[4] Stamps	Medicaid	Social Security	Federal[4] Income	State Income	Work[5] Expenses	"Disposable" Income
0	0	$5,052	$2,166	Yes	0	0	0	0	$9,522[6]
$2,000	$346	4,982	1,854	Yes	$153	0	0	$600	10,643
4,000	692	3,292	1,974	Yes	306	0	0	1,200	10,756
5,000	865	2,492	2,034	Yes	383	0	0	1,500	10,812
6,000	1,038	1,692	2,094	Yes	459	0	0	1,800	10,869
7,000	1,211	892	2,154	Yes	536	0	0	2,100	10,925
8,000	1,235	0	2,241	Yes[7]	612	0	0	2,400	10,768
9,000	1,235	0	2,061	Yes[8]	689	0	$38	2,700	11,173
10,000	1,235	0	1,881	No[8]	765	0	210	3,000	11,445
15,000	772	0	0	No[9]	1,148	0	315	4,200	10,109
20,000	154	0	0	No	1,530	$283	420	5,200	12,721
30,000	0	0	0	No	2,295	1,943	630	5,400	19,732
50,000	0	0	0	No	3,825	6,405	1,050	5,400	33,320

Notes:

1. Assumes that both children are over age 1. If one were younger, EITC would be larger (maximum of $1,592 at earnings of $8,000-$10,000).

2. Assumes these deductions: $120 monthly standard allowance (which would drop to $90 after 1 year on the job) and child care costs equal to 20 percent of earnings, up to maximum of $350 for 2 children.

3. Assumes these deductions: 20 percent of earnings, $116 monthly standard deduction and child care costs equal to 20 percent of wages, up to maximum of $320 for 2 children.

4. Head of household rates in effect for 1991. The dependent care tax credit reduces tax liability at earnings of $15,000 and above. Under IRS rules, unless earnings at least equal AFDC, the mother generally is not a "head of household" eligible for EITC; but it appears that this rule is rarely applied. Example assumes the rule is not applied.

5. Assumed to equal 10 percent of earnings up to maximum of $100 monthly, plus child care costs equal to 20 percent of earnings up to the maximum allowed by AFDC ($350 for 2 children).

6. The benefits from Medicaid are added. In Pennsylvania, the cost of Medicaid for a 3-person AFDC family averaged about $2,304 in fiscal year 1989.

7. Family would qualify for Medicaid because the mother, by law, would be deemed still an AFDC recipient, even though no AFDC would be paid; her calculated benefit would be below the minimum amount ($10 monthly) payable.

8. Family would qualify for Medicaid for 12 months after leaving AFDC under the 1988 Family Support Act. State must offer Medicaid to all children up to age 6 whose family income is not above 133 percent of the Federal poverty guideline (ceiling of $14,850 for a family of 3 in 1991) and to children over age 6 born after September 1, 1983 (up to age 7 1/3 in January 1991), whose family income is below the poverty guideline ($11,140 for a family of 3).

9. After losing her Medicaid transitional benefits, to regain eligibility, mother must spend down on medical expenses to State's medically needy income limit ($5,400 in September 1989).

This table is adapted from the one in US House of Representatives, Greenbook (1992), page 590. Data source: Congressional Research Service.

TABLE 8
Caseloads for 8 Large Federal Programs (millions)

Program	1975	1980	1990
AFDC (total recipients)	11.1	10.6	11.2
(child recipients)	8.0	7.3	7.6
Food stamps (total recipients)	16.3	19.2	20.0
Medicaid (total recipients)	22.0	21.6	25.3
(child recipients)	9.6	9.3	11.2
Housing Assistance (#households)	3.2[1]	4.0	5.4
WIC (# women)	.2[1]	.4	1.0
(# infants)	.2	.5	1.4
(# children)	.5	1.0	2.1
School Lunch (# any meals)	26.3[1]	26.6	12.8
(# with free meals)	10.5	10.0	10.3
Head Start	.4	.4	.6
Earned Income Tax Credit			
(# families)	6.2	7.0	13.3

Notes:
1. These figures are for 1977.

Table 7 shows the benefits that a Pennsylvania mother with two children would receive from AFDC, Food Stamps, Medicaid, and the EITC given various levels of earned income. Even for a mother with no earned income, AFDC benefits would make up only 53% of family income. The proportion would decline to 23% for a mother earning $5,000. The table illustrates the work disincentives created by the welfare system: two mothers who earned between $2,000 and $8,000 would have very similar levels of disposable income. And a mother who increased her earnings from $7,000 to $8,000 would actually suffer a decrease in disposable income of $157. because of the loss of AFDC benefits, while a mother who increased her earnings from $7,000 to $10,000 would lose her Medicaid coverage (valued using the average Medicaid expenditure in Pennsylvania of $2,304 in this example), as well as her AFDC benefits, for a net loss of $1,784.[23]

B. Trends In Caseloads and Expenditures

Table 8 shows the caseloads of these programs in 1975, 1980, and 1990.

---

[23] There is considerable debate about whether the linkage between Medicaid and AFDC provides a significant incentive for women to stay on welfare. The first paper to look into this issue (Blank (1989) did not find any significant effect. More recently, Yelowitz (1993) does find a positive relationship between the generosity of Medicaid and AFDC recipiency.

TABLE 9
Trends in Program Expenditures (billions 1990 $)[1]

Program	1975	1980	1990
AFDC (total)	20.4	19.0	18.5
(federal only)	11.2	10.2	10.1
Food stamps	10.2[2]	13.8	15.1
Medicaid (total)	30.6	40.9	72.5
(federal only)	17.2	23.2	41.1
(to dependent children)	5.4	5.1[3]	9.1
(to adults in families with dependent children)	5.1	5.5[3]	8.6
Housing Assistance	6.3[4]	8.6	10.6
WIC	.6[4]	.7	2.1
School Lunch	4.5[4]	4.8	3.7
Head Start	1.0	1.1	1.6
Earned Income Tax Credit (total)	3.2	3.2	6.9
(refunded portion of credit)	2.2	2.2	5.3
Total:	76.8	94.3	131.0

Notes:
1. These figures were taken from the US House of Representatives, Greenbook (1992), pages 654, 1019, 1616, 1651, 1680, 1684, 1689, and 1695.
2. The figure for 1975 includes administrative costs. The figures for 1980 and 1990 do not.
3. These figures are for 1981.
4. These figures are for 1977.

Over the past 15 years, the number of children served by AFDC has actually declined slightly. Caseloads of the Food Stamps program and Medicaid showed modest growth. The number of households receiving housing assistance, and the number of children in Head Start, grew by 69% and 50%, respectively. But the programs that have shown the greatest growth in caseload are WIC and EITC. These programs grew by 400% and 115%, respectively.

The trends in program expenditures are documented in Table 9. Despite the fact that the maximum AFDC benefit for a family of four in the median state fell by 33% between 1975 and 1990, expenditures on AFDC have declined only slightly faster than the caseload. Since two 2-person families are more expensive than a single 4-person family, these figures may reflect a shift in the composition of the caseload towards smaller families. In contrast, average monthly Food Stamp benefits increased by 27% per person over the same period, resulting in a 50% increase in expenditures. Expenditures on Medicaid rose dramatically, although caseloads grew only slowly. This increase in Medicaid costs reflects an increase in the cost per visit that is also occurring in the non-Medicaid population (Newhouse, 1992). Expenditures on Head Start and housing assistance increased at roughly the same pace as the caseload. Expenditures on WIC and the EITC doubled, but given the explosion in WIC caseloads, expenditures per participant were roughly halved. The only in-kind program to show a decline in expenditures was the National School Lunch Program – expenditures fell by 18% in real terms.

These trends are summarized in Figure 5. The figure shows that in 1975 cash transfers from AFDC made up 35% of the support provided to families with children. By 1990, this fraction had dropped to 19%. The intervening 15 years saw an increase of 57% in the amount of aid provided in the form of specific in-kind services and tax credits. The most spectacular increases were in WIC and EITC, two programs in which benefits are conditional on socially approved behavior: WIC participants must undergo counseling, medical examinations, and buy specific food stuffs, while EITC claimants must work.

C. Do Welfare Programs Raise Children out of Poverty?

i) Definition of Poverty

The poverty line is an extremely arbitrary indicator of well-being. It was developed by Mollie Orshansky of the Department of Agriculture in the mid-1960s. The poverty level was originally calculated by determining the minimum amount of money necessary to purchase a 'nutritionally adequate' diet and multiplying this number by 3, since surveys had indicated that families generally spent about one-third of their income on food. In recent years, the poverty level has been updated each year by increasing the previous year's threshold using the change in the Consumer Price Index. In 1990, the poverty threshold for a family of 4 persons was $13,359.

The use of the official poverty line as a measure of welfare has been severely criticized. For example, Slesnick (1993) attacks the use of a pre-tax measure of income rather than a measure of consumption. Nevertheless, the fact that the poverty line is an imperfect measure does not make it a useless one. It has been consistently defined over a long period of time and a great deal of detailed information about poverty rates for various groups is available. It is used as a benchmark in this section.

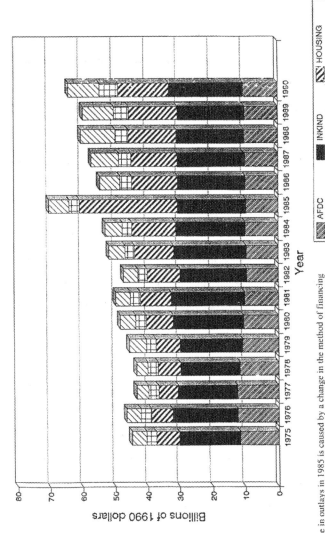

FIGURE 5   Federal welfare expenditures.

Note: The bulge in outlays in 1985 is caused by a change in the method of financing public housing, which generated close to $14 billion in one-time expenditures. This amount paid off—all at once—the capital cost of public housing construction and modernization activities undertaken between 1974 and 1985, which otherwise would have been paid off over periods of up to 40 years. Because of this one-time expenditure, however, future outlays for public housing will be lower than they would have been otherwise.

ii) The Anti-Poverty Effectiveness of Welfare Programs

Figure 6 shows that in most states, the combined AFDC and Food Stamp benefit is less than the poverty line. Hence, these programs do not raise families on welfare from poverty. Nevertheless, the evidence suggests that poverty rates would be even higher in the absence of the welfare system. Table 10 shows the sources of income of families in the bottom and top quintiles of the income distribution. The first half of the table focuses on all families with children. The figures in the table are expressed as percentages of the poverty line.

The first line of the table shows that private income from family earnings and other sources brought the average family in the lowest quintile up to 62% of the poverty line in 1979. Among poor families with children, 63% reported that some members of the household worked, although only 27% had the equivalent of a full-time worker in 1990. The corresponding figures for poor female-headed families were 51% and 13%, respectively.[24]

In 1979, cash transfer income raised the income of families in the lowest quintile to 85% of the poverty line, while non-cash transfers raised it a further 11%, to 96% of poverty. After subtracting out taxes, the average family with children in the lowest quintile had an income of 93% of the poverty line.

The second line of the table shows that in 1989, the contributions of private income and cash transfers to the lowest quintile fell. However, these losses were offset by gains in noncash transfers and in tax relief, leaving the average family in the lowest quintile with an income of 87% of the poverty line. In contrast, the incomes of the highest quintile rose between 1979 and 1989, relative to the poverty line.

The second half of the table shows similar figures for female-headed households. Once again, increases in noncash transfers and tax credits partially offset reductions in earnings and cash transfers. If female heads were unable to make up any lost welfare income through increased earnings, then one could conclude that the welfare system raised the incomes of the average female-headed household in the lowest quintile from 15% of the poverty line to 47% of the poverty line in 1989. This is a strong assumption but it seems equally arbitrary to suppose that the average welfare mother could increase her earnings to 47% of the poverty line in the absence of any trans-

---

[24] Moffitt (1990) reports that female heads are as likely to work as other women, and that they have slightly higher earnings. Thus, in most cases, the poverty of these families is associated with the absence of support from the father of the children.

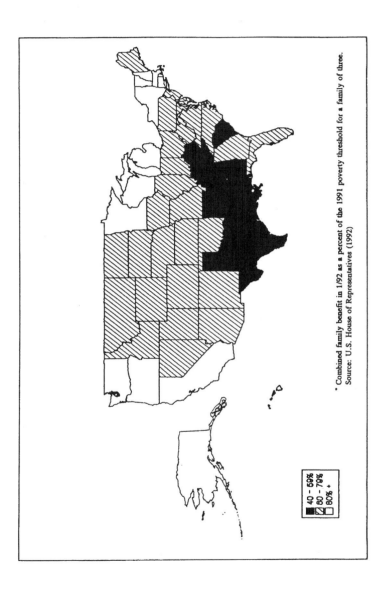

* Combined family benefit in 1/92 as a percent of the 1991 poverty threshold for a family of three.
Source: U.S. House of Representatives (1992)

FIGURE 6   Maximum combined AFDC and Food Stamp Benefit as a percent of poverty for a one-parent family of three, January 1992*

TABLE 10
Sources of Average Posttax Income[1]

Income quintile and year	Total private income[2]	Cash transfer income		Pretax cash adjusted income[5]	Means-tested noncash transfers[6]	Taxes[7]	Post-tax adjusted income[8]
		Non-means tested cash[3]	Means-tested cash[4]				
All Families with Children, by Income Quintile, 1979 and 1989							
Lowest :							
1979	0.618	0.079	0.153	0.850	0.114	-0.035	0.929
1989	.552	.063	.137	.752	.134	-.015	.871
Change	-.066	-.016	-.016	-.098	.020	.020	-.058
% Change	-10.6	-20.6	-10.2	-11.5	17.1	-58.3	-6.2
Highest:							
1979	6.063	.063	.014	6.140	.006	-1.210	4.936
1989	7.108	.077	.003	7.188	.003	-1.396	5.795
Change	1.045	.014	-.011	1.048	-.003	-.186	.859
% Change	17.2	22.5	-77.9	17.1	-45.0	15.4	17.4
Total:							
1979	2.998	.074	.053	3.125	.036	-.491	2.670
1989	3.258	.079	.039	3.376	.037	-.532	2.881
Change	.260	.005	-.014	.251	.001	-.041	.211
% Change	8.7	7.0	-26.0	8.0	1.9	8.2	7.9
Single Mothers with Children, by Income Quintile, 1979 and 1989							
Lowest:							
1979	0.149	0.038	0.172	0.359	0.137	-0.005	0.491
1989	.132	.025	.140	.296	.166	.004	.466
Change	-.017	-.013	-.032	-.063	.028	.009	-.025
%Change	-11.7	-33.7	-18.8	-17.4	20.8	-176.0	-5.2
Highest:							
1979	3.334	.239	.064	3.637	.023	-.450	3.210
1989	3.938	.185	.013	4.135	.011	-.550	3.596
Change	.604	-.054	-.051	.498	-.012	-.100	.386
% Change	18.1	-22.7	-80.0	13.7	-52.6	22.2	12.0
Total:							
1979	1.268	.125	.198	1.591	.123	-.133	1.581
1989	1.404	.095	.143	1.642	.129	-.140	1.631
Change	.136	-.030	-.055	.051	.006	-.007	.050
% Change	0.7	-23.7	-27.9	3.2	4.8	5.6	3.1

Notes:
1. This table is adapted from the one in US House of Representatives, Greenbook (1992), page 1395.
2. Total private income: total family earnings plus income from private pensions, military or government retirement, annuities, and other retirement programs; interest income, dividends, rents, royalties, and other income from investments; all other income from private sources including child support and alimony payments and other forms of cash income from non-government sources.

3. Non-mean-tested cash transfers: Social Security income (payments from the old age, survivors, and disability insurance program); railroad retirement income; and other Gorvernment cash transfers that are not awarded on the basis of income level, including unemployment compensation, workers'compensation, veterans' benefits, and other transfers.

4. Means tested cash transfers: Government cash transfers that are awarded on the basis of income level, including aid to families with dependent children (AFDC), supplemental security income (SSI), and general assistance.

5. Pretax cash AFI: total private income plus non-means-tested cash transfers plus means-tested cash transfers.

6. Means-tested noncash transfers: the cash equivalent of food and housing assistance provided to low-income families, including food stamps, school lunches, public housing, and housing subsidies.

7. Taxes: Federal individual income and employee payroll taxes.

8. Posttax AFI: total pretax cash AFI plus means-tested noncash transfers minus taxes.

fers. The safest conclusion is that an increase in income of 32% of the poverty line represents an upper bound on the anti-poverty effect of the welfare system.

D. Spending on Children Compared to Spending on the Elderly

Another useful way to put spending on children into perspective, is to compare it to spending on another vulnerable group. Table 11 shows total expenditures on the elderly in 1990. A comparison of Tables 5 and 11 indicates that the government spends much more on the elderly than on children. In fact, the federal government spends only $1,020 per child under 18 compared to $11,350 per elderly person. Of course, these estimates do not take state and local expenditures on education into account. The biggest components of federal spending on the elderly are Social Security and Medicare which are projected to rise to $261 billion and $156 billion, respectively, by 1995.

Figure 7 compares child poverty rates to those of all Americans and to those of the elderly. Since 1975, child poverty rates have exceeded those of the elderly and the gap has been increasing over time. The gap is not surprising when we consider that of the 50 million individuals who would have been poor in the absence of transfer programs in 1990, 17.5 million were raised from poverty by Social Security, while only 6.7 million were raised from poverty by means-tested cash, food, or housing benefits.[25]

---

[25] These estimates were computed by Mathematica Policy Research, Inc. from the Survey of Income and Program Participation and are reported in US House of Representatives (1992, p.1342).

TABLE 11

Estimated Federal Spending for the Elderly under Selected Programs,
Fiscal Years 1965-1990 (billions 1990 dollars)

Program	1965	1971	1975	1980	1985	1990
Social Security	(¹)	82.6	122.9	130.3	169.5	192.7
Railroad Retirement	(¹)	5.2	6.6	5.8	5.7	3.4
Federal civilian retirement	(¹)	7.0	13.0	12.5	16.5	22.8
Military retirement	(¹)	2.1	2.6	2.9	5.2	7.4
Benefits for coal miners[2]	(¹)	.3	.5	2.1	1.8	1.3
Supplemental Security Income[3]	(¹)	4.3	4.3	3.7	3.9	3.3
Veterans pensions[4]	(¹)	2.7	3.6	5.3	6.5	7.4
Medicare	(¹)	22.9	30.3	47.0	74.1	95.4
Medicaid	(¹)	5.8	6.2	7.5	10.3	16.2
Food Stamps[5]	(¹)	.6	2.4	.8	.7	1.1
Housing Assistance[6]	(¹)	.6	1.0	3.7	4.5	5.2
Total (1990 dollars)[7]	71.3	134.1	192.9	221.6	299.7	356.2
Total (current dollars)	18.8	44.0	81.3	138.1	248.3	356.2

Notes:

1. Estimated total spending for the elderly in 1965 was taken from a source that did not report spending separately by program.

2. Prior to 1980, represents benefits for miners' widows only.

3. 1970 estimate represents grants to states for aid to the aged, blind and disabled.

4. Includes other veterans' compensation beginning in 1980.

5. Includes nutrition assistance to Puerto Rico.

6. Adjusted to eliminate outlays resulting from changing the financing procedures for public housing.

7. Conversion to 1990 dollars used fiscal averages for the CPI-X1.

Sources: Figures for 1990 calculated by the Congressional Budget Office. Program spending figures for 1971 - 85 from the 1986 Statistical Abstract of the United States. Total spending on the aged for 1965 from R. Clark and J. Menefee (1981).

Poverty measures are based only on cash income and exclude in-kind transfers such as Food Stamps, Medicaid, and Medicare as well as the imputed value of owner-occupied housing. Since the elderly have received the lion's share of increased federal and state spending on medical care and are more likely to own their own homes than families with children, official poverty rates understate the extent to which the economic status of children and the elderly has diverged (Preston, 1984). The rise in child poverty is even more remarkable when we consider that more mothers contribute to family income than ever before.

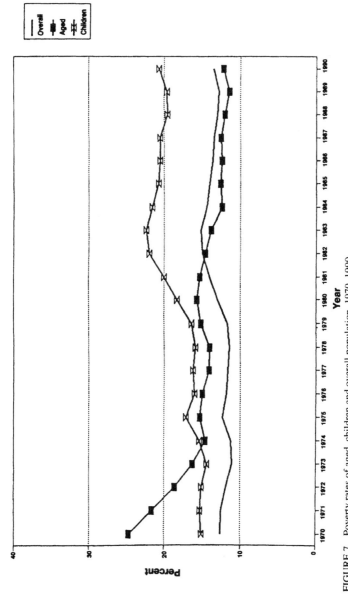

FIGURE 7   Poverty rates of aged, children and overall population, 1970–1990.

Source: U.S. House Representatives (1992).

TABLE 12
Distribution of Persons by Adjusted Income

Country	Children % Poor	Children % Near Poor	Elderly % Poor	Elderly % Near Poor
United States	21.4	9.0	24.6	11.5
Australia	15.4	8.6	14.9	30.3
Canada	15.2	9.1	18.5	18.6
Netherlands	8.0	10.5	3.4	3.2
Switzerland	7.3	8.4	11.4	16.1
United Kingdom	9.3	9.7	34.7	21.7
Israel	10.8	12.8	25.0	14.3
Germany	2.8	8.5	11.8	13.6
Norway	5.0	5.8	5.5	24.7
Sweden	5.2	4.6	1.1	10.4
Simple Mean	10.0	8.7	15.1	16.4

Source: J. Coder, L. Rainwater, and T. Smeeding (1989).

Table 12 provides an international comparison of poverty rates among children and the elderly. Poor persons here are defined as those living in families with incomes less than half the median income. The near-poor are defined as those in families with incomes between 50% and 62.5% of the median income. The table indicates that children in the United States are more likely to be poor or near-poor than children in any of the other countries. In contrast, American elderly are no more likely to be poor or near-poor than elderly people in Australia, the United Kingdom, or Israel, although they are more likely to be poor than the average elderly person in the other countries considered.

E. Summary

The largest federal programs for children are AFDC, Food Stamps, and Medicaid. Expenditures on AFDC have fallen over time, expenditures on Food Stamps have risen somewhat, and expenditures on Medicaid have shot up due to the increasing costs of medical care for a relatively stable caseload. Since 1975, the fastest growing programs in terms of both caseloads and expenditures have been WIC, and the Earned Income Tax Credit, which can be thought of as a transfer program for working parents. Head Start also showed rapid growth. These patterns demonstrate the shift away from unrestricted transfers in the form of AFDC payments towards more restricted transfers and programs targeted directly to children.

Federal anti-poverty programs have not been effective in reducing the percentage of children in poverty. A comparison of expenditures on children to expenditures on the elderly suggests that one reason for this failure may be that expenditures on children are relatively small. This analysis raises the question of whether tax payers may be more willing to pay for programs targeted to working parents or directly to children than they have been to pay for programs such as AFDC?

Part 2: Evaluation of Individual Programs

The chapters in this section each focus on the evaluation of a particular program. Chapters 4, 5, and 6 discuss Aid for Families with Dependent Children (AFDC), Medicaid, and the Food Stamp Program, respectively. Supplemental feeding programs are discussed in Chapter 7, Chapter 8 provides an overview of Head Start, and Chapter 9 deals with public housing. Chapter 10 examines tax credits for working families and Chapter 11 concludes.

The results reviewed below suggest first that cash income from AFDC has much the same effect on children as cash income from any other source. There is no evidence that AFDC participation *per se* is harmful to children. But there is also no evidence that the benefits of public expenditures on AFDC accrue mainly to children. In contrast, Chapter 5 suggests that the utilization of care and some health outcomes may be improved by expanding the health insurance coverage of poor children under the Medicaid program.

Evaluations of the Food Stamp Program (a 'near-cash' program) yield contradictory and inconclusive findings. In contrast, the evidence suggests that supplemental feeding programs like WIC, NSLP, and SBP, which direct specific benefits directly to the intended recipients can improve pregnancy outcomes and child nutrition.

Participation in Head Start is associated with better performance on standardized tests among whites and Hispanics. Perhaps more importantly, white and Hispanic children are less likely to have repeated a grade if they attended Head Start and white children are more likely to receive measles shots. In contrast, African-Americans who attended Head Start do not appear to perform better on tests or in school. They do, however, seem to do better in terms of health: they are more likely to receive measles shots and are significantly taller than their siblings who did not attend a preschool.

Despite the fact that housing constitutes the single largest expenditure of most families, little is known about the effects of housing on child health and well-being. And although the subject has been much researched, the effects of neighborhoods and schools on children's prospects remain controversial. However, the available evidence does suggest that a dollar spent on voucher programs is likely to have a more positive impact than a dollar spent on the construction on new public housing.

Finally, Chapter 10 emphasizes the parallels between the EITC and the Negative Income Tax program. The NIT experiments provide the strongest evidence we have that transfers to parents can have measurable positive effects on children. Transfers to the poorest families appear to improve children's school performance and nutritional status. Families also upgrade their housing in response to transfers – a change that may have a large impact on children's lives.

4. AFDC

Chapter 3 showed that although AFDC is one of the oldest and largest federal welfare programs, declining real benefit levels in most states suggest that it enjoys little popular support. There seems to be a widespread consensus that AFDC does not work as it should. Yet this chapter will show that we know very little about the effects of AFDC on the children who are its intended beneficiaries.

Most research on AFDC has focused on work disincentives, the durations of spells of AFDC receipt, effects on family structure, incentives for family migration, or the intergenerational transmission of welfare dependency (Moffitt, 1992). Of this list, studies of family structure (in particular, of incentives for teenage child bearing) and of the intergenerational transmission of welfare dependency are the only ones that deal directly with the effects of AFDC participation on children.

In this chapter, we discuss the handful of studies that examine the influence of AFDC on children's cognitive achievement, as well as studies of the intergenerational transmission of welfare dependency, and of the influence of AFDC on teenage pregnancy and child bearing. None of the studies reviewed here establish a causal link between AFDC and the limited number of outcomes examined.

A. Effects of AFDC on Young Children

Before evaluating the literature linking child development and AFDC, it is useful to outline the ways that maternal AFDC participation might affect children. The most direct pathway is through increased income since there is a well-established link between family income and cognitive achievement. However, if mothers reduce their work effort in order to take advantage of the AFDC program, then AFDC participation may not increase income above what it otherwise would have been.[26]

In any case, it is possible that AFDC participation has effects over and above any effect on income. On the positive side, a single mother who is able to stay home with her children may be able to offer them more attention than one who works. On the negative side, a mother on AFDC may suffer from low motivation or self-esteem and may transmit these attitudes to her child (Murray, 1984). There is little direct evidence about either of these propositions. But they suggest that it would be enlightening to see if AFDC has any effect other than through its effect on income.

Currie and Cole (1993) use data from the 1979 to 1988 waves of the National Longitudinal Survey of Youth (NLSY) to examine the effect of participation in AFDC during pregnancy on birthweight. They find that participation has a negative effect in OLS regressions, but when selection into the programs is controlled for using either instrumental variables techniques or sibling differences, no significant effects are found.[27]

They are also unable to find any effect of AFDC participation on the probability of initiating prenatal care in the first trimester of pregnancy once observed and unobserved characteristics of the mothers are controlled for. Their conclusions contrast with those of Coburn and McDonald (1992), for example, who found that in 1985 and 1986, women were more likely to have adequate prenatal care in high AFDC benefit states than in low AFDC benefit states. The discrepancy suggests that women in high benefit states differ from those in low benefit states in ways that affect their utilizations of prenatal care.

---

[26] As Moffitt (1992) notes, most studies have found little effect of AFDC benefits on work effort. However, Hoynes and MacCurdy (1993) argue that higher benefits are associated with longer welfare spells.

[27] In a study of poor women that did not take account of selection into the program, Moss and Carver (1993) also find that participation in Medicaid during pregnancy and during infancy is associated with increases in infant mortality rates.

Using data from the National Longitudinal Survey's Child-Mother file
(NLSCM), Hill and O'Neill (1992) examine the effects of maternal AFDC
participation on the PPVT scores of 4-year-old children, controlling for
income. This is apparently the only paper that examines the direct effect of
AFDC receipt on children's cognitive attainment. The welfare measure used
is the proportion of years the mother received AFDC after age 18. This
variable has a strong negative effect in OLS regressions that disappears
when the welfare measure is instrumented using a list of variables that includes state-level measures of available AFDC and Food Stamp benefits,
state level average wages, and unemployment rates in the local labor market. These results indicate that the negative effect of the number of years the
mother was on welfare in the OLS regressions reflects other unobserved
characteristics of the mother rather than a true AFDC effect.

A related line of research deals with the effects of maternal employment
on children's well-being. Presumably, in the absence of the AFDC program,
some children's mothers would be forced to work. Hence, an assessment of
the effects of maternal employment provides indirect evidence about the
effects of AFDC. Unfortunately, much of this research focuses on middle-
class families, which limits its applicability to the question at hand.[28]

However, two recent papers address the issue using the NLSCM. Since
this data set oversamples poor, minority women, the results of these studies
may have more bearing on the effects of AFDC. Desai et al. (1989) focus on
the PPVT scores of 4-year-old children from the 1986 wave of the survey,
while Blau and Grossberg (1990) use PPVT scores of 3- and 4-year-old
children. Both studies report that maternal employment in the first year has
a negative effect on boys. But when Blau and Grossberg instrument employment using characteristics of the mother and spouse they do not find
any significant effect of employment.[29]

Haveman, Wolfe and Spaulding (1991) use data from the Panel Study of
Income Dynamics to show that the time a mother spent on AFDC while the
child was an adolescent is negatively correlated with high school completion while the time she spent working is positively associated with high
school completion. They do not attempt to control for selection into either
AFDC or employment.

---

[28] See Desai et al., (1989) for a brief survey of this literature. Most of these papers make no
attempt to control for unobserved factors that might be correlated with the mother's decision to
return to work.

[29] These results must be viewed with caution since it is not clear that any of the variables
used as instruments can be legitimately excluded from the PPVT equation.

TABLE 13
OLS Estimates of the Effects of Maternal AFDC
Participation on Children's Cognitive Attainment

White

	Piat math	Piat reading comprehension	Piat reading recognition	PPVT	Ever repeated a grade
% of Child's Life Mother on AFDC	-7.97 (-2.82)	-11.10 (-3.23)	-8.29 (-2.86)	-5.38 (-1.82)	0.32 (2.94)
Permanent Income	4.91 (3.19)	4.82 (2.61)	5.57 (3.55)	5.75 (3.76)	-0.01) (-0.13)
R-Squared	0.19	0.20	0.21	0.23	0.15
# Observations	1504	1133	1491	1863	298

African-American

	Piat math	Piat reading comprehension	Piat reading recognition	PPVT	Ever repeated a grade
% of Child's Life Mother on AFDC	-0.24 (-0.10)	-0.27 (-0.10)	-3.58 (-1.49)	-2.62 (-1.48)	-0.09 (-0.93)
Permanent Income	5.39) (3.14)	5.63) (2.93)	5.28 (3.00)	3.40 (2.69)	-0.10 (-1.45)
R-Squared	0.12	0.22	0.18	0.17	0.10
# Observations	1037	834	1021	1152	292

Notes: statistics in parentheses.
   Other variables included in the model are whether the child is a male or the firstborn, child's birthweight, mother's AFQT score, grandmother's highest grade obtained, whether the mother lived in an urban area at age 14, whether a working adult male lived in the home when the mother was 14, county population, county per capita income, child's age in 1990, and a dummy for whether this age is over 5.
   The PIAT tests were administered to children 5 years of age and older. The PPVT test was administered to children 3 years of age and older. If there is more than one score per child, we take the average score in order to attenuate the influence of random measurement error.
   The question about repeating a grade was only asked to children over 10-years-old. Permanent income equals the mean income between 1978 and 1990 in 1990 dollars.

Table 13 shows some additional OLS estimates of the effects of maternal AFDC receipt on cognitive achievement. These models are also estimated · using the NLSCM. PPVT and PIAT scores as well as a variable equal to one if the child has ever repeated a grade are included as dependent variables.

TABLE 14
Estimates of the Effects of Maternal AFDC
Participation on Children's Cognitive Attainment Based on
Model that Include Mother Fixed Effects

	Piat math	Piat reading comprehension	Piat reading recognition	PPVT	Ever failed a grade
Regression 1					
% of Child's Life Mother on AFDC	-5.37 (-0.56)	14.91 (0.96)	29.65 (2.86)	1.60 (0.22)	-5.07 (-3.17)
Income	0.02 (0.01)	1.18 (0.53)	1.48 (0.90)	1.09 (0.88)	-0.47 (-1.25)
Male	-1.62 (-1.52)	-4.22 (-2.97)	-5.77 (-5.14)	-2.07 (-2.35)	0.06 (0.62)
First Born	-0.59 (-0.43)	2.52 (1.33)	1.18 (0.81)	1.27 (0.22)	0.08 (0.64)
Birthweight	0.09 (2.76)	0.04 (0.84)	0.05 (1.53)	0.05 (1.96)	-0.00 (-0.68)
Child Age	0.07 (2.18)	-0.08 (-1.54)	0.10 (2.90)	0.16 (6.33)	-0.01 (-1.86)
R-Squared	0.71	0.74	0.71	0.79	0.83
#Observations	2397	1595	2358	2995	330
#Mother Fixed Effects	1209	864	1192	1475	242
Regression 2					
% of Child's Life Mother on AFDC	-17.60 (-1.58)	-7.41 (-0.40)	13.48 (1.15)	-0.10 (-0.01)	0.26 (0.12)
Income	-0.79 (-0.46)	-0.07 (0.03)	1.65 (0.92)	0.66 (0.49)	-0.55 (0.49)
Male	-1.61 (-1.36)	-4.36 (-2.63)	-5.01 (-4.04)	-1.79 (-1.88)	-1.79 (-1.88)
First Born	-1.02 (-0.65)	2.33 (1.04)	2.44 (1.49)	-0.59 (-0.47)	-0.59 (-0.47)
Birthweight	0.10 (2.59)	0.03 (0.47)	0.05 (1.34)	0.05 (1.60)	0.05 (1.60)

TABLE 14 (Continued)

	Piat math	Piat reading comprehension	Piat reading recognition	PPVT	Ever failed a grade
Child Age	-0.48	-0.52	-1.68	1.97	-0.11
	(-0.23)	(-0.18)	(-0.77)	(1.17)	(-0.56)
Spouse in	1.44	0.83	0.77	-2.18	0.05
Birth Year	(0.75)	(0.30)	(0.39)	(-1.42)	(0.15)
Employment in	2.65	4.96	0.23	0.89	-0.31
Birth Year	(1.67)	(2.25)	(0.14)	(0.70)	(-0.66)
Mother Age in	0.03	-0.15	-0.06	0.33	-0.16
Birth Year	(0.16)	(-0.58)	(-0.33)	(2.32)	(-0.87)
R-Squared	0.74	0.78	0.73	0.81	0.97
#Observations	2121	1348	2086	2697	197
#Mother Fixed Effects	1154	803	1137	1419	173

Notes:
   Income is mean of income in year before birth, birth year, and year after birth in 1990 dollars. Statistics in parentheses.

The measure of AFDC is the percentage of the *child's* life that the mother received AFDC. This is arguably a better measure of the child's 'exposure' to AFDC, and is less likely to reflect the mother's background than total years of maternal welfare receipt. All models control for the permanent income of the household (defined as the mean real income from 1978 to 1990) as well as the additional characteristics of mother and child that are listed in the table notes. Estimates are shown separately for whites and African-Americans.

   These estimates suggest that exposure to AFDC has a negative effect on the cognitive achievement of white children. But there are no statistically significant effects of exposure to AFDC on the test scores or schooling attainment of African-American children. Since the gap in socio-economic status between white children on AFDC and the average white child is much greater than the gap for African-American children, this racial difference may indicate that the negative effect for whites reflects selection into the program rather than a causal effect of AFDC.

This issue is explored further in Table 14. This table presents estimates of the effects of AFDC exposure that include a fixed effect for each mother. Hence, we are comparing children in the same family who differ in terms of the length of time they have been exposed to AFDC. The idea is that if AFDC causes low achievement, then longer exposures should be more harmful. By comparing siblings, we eliminate all constant, family-specific sources of differences between children.

The first part of the table shows that even when differences in income in the birth year, gender, birth order, birthweight, and age are controlled or, exposure to AFDC has a slight positive effect. Children with longer exposures are estimated to have significantly higher PIAT Reading Recognition scores and significaintly lower probabilities of repeating a grade than siblings with shorter exposures. In the second part of Table 14, differences in marital and employment status in the birth year, as well as mother's age at the birth are also controlled for. Since changes in AFDC status are likely to be related to changes in these variables, it is not clear that they should be included in the models. When they are, differences in exposure to AFDC have no effect: this result illustrates the difficulties involved in distinguishing between the effects of AFDC and the effects of family structure.

The safest conclusion on the basis of the scant available evidence, is that AFDC exposure does not have either strong positive or strong negative effects on cognitive development. In other words, a dollar of income from AFDC has much the same effect on a child as a dollar of family income from other sources. The absence of a strong positive effect of AFDC (conditional on income) is consistent with the fact that maternal employment has not been shown to have harmful effects.

B. Intergenerational Transmission of Poverty and Welfare Dependency

Much of the research about the effects of AFDC on children, focuses on the question of whether daughters of women who participate in AFDC are themselves more likely to participate. This link is called the intergenerational transmission of welfare dependency. Critics of the welfare system point to intergenerational transmission as evidence that parental welfare participation actually harms poor children by affecting their aspirations (cf. Charles Murray (1984)). However, an assessment of the extent to which poverty is transmitted from one generation to the next should logically precede a discussion of welfare dependency, because the fact that women whose mothers were on AFDC are more likely than other women to be on AFDC, may simply be a reflection of the fact that the children of the poor are likely to be poor. Both questions are addressed in this section.

i) Is Poverty Transmitted from One Generation to the Next?

Some controversy exists about the extent to which poverty is transmitted from one generation to the next. On the one hand, authors like Harrington (1962, p. 21) claim that 'the real explanation of why the poor are where they are is that they made the mistake of being born to the wrong parents. . . . On the other hand, Jencks *et al.* (1972), Behrman and Taubman (1985), and Becker (1988) argue that family background has only a small effect, since correlations between the earnings of brothers, or between the earnings of fathers and sons, are typically no greater than .2 at any point in time.

In a series of papers, Solon (1992), Solon *et al.* (1988, 1991), Corcoran et al. (1989) and Zimmerman (1992), criticize two aspects of the previous studies. First, some of these studies rely on very homogeneous samples: for example, Behrman and Taubman's sample of fathers is composed of white male twins who both served in the military. Studies with very homogeneous samples will tend to under-estimate the true correlation between siblings or between generations. The basic problem is that in a sample in which all members resemble each other, the relationships between relatives do not stand out.

A second problem is that most previous studies use income measured at a point in time. Since the incomes of individuals are subject to transitory shocks and are often measured with error, the correlation between the incomes of two relatives at a point in time is likely to be lower than the correlation between their average incomes over a longer period.

In less homogeneous samples, the correlation in permanent income between fathers and sons is at least .4, or double the previous estimates. Hence, there does seem to be a substantial degree of correlation between the incomes of parents and children.

ii) Intergenerational Transmission of AFDC Participation

Given the fact that there is intergenerational transmission of poverty, it is not surprising that daughters of mothers who receive AFDC are more likely to receive AFDC themselves.[30] Several studies that make this point are sum-

JANET CURRIE

TABLE 15

Studies of the Intergenerational Transmission of Welfare and Poverty[1]

Study	Data set	Population	Dependent variable	Independent variable	Estimating technique	Results
Rein and Rainwater (1978)	PSID, 1968–77	Women 18–54 in 1968	Female heads with children: on welfare in early years as head of household	Parental family on welfare in 1967 and 1968	Simple correlations	No increase in probability of daughter being on welfare after controlling for parental income
Levy (1980)	PSID, 1968–76	Women 10–17 in 1968 living at home	Single and on welfare	Parental family on welfare in 1968	Logit	Weak pos. effect
Hill-Ponza (1983)	PSID, 1968–81	Children 12–17 in 1968 and living home	Daughters: ratio of welfare income to total income after leaving home	Ratio of welfare income to total income of parental family prior to leaving home	Probit Adjusted OLS	Daughters: generally (+) but weak effect on prob. of receiving any welfare
Lerman (1986)	NLSY 1979–81	Black sons 16–23 in 1980 living at home	Earnings in 1980; whether out of school and at work	Family received welfare in 1980	OLS, Probit	(-), Sig. earnings effects (+) Sig. non-school-work effects. Effects weaken or disappear if predicted or disappear if predicted family variable used

TABLE 15 (Continued)

Study	Data set	Population	Dependent variable	Independent variable	Estimating technique	Results
McLanahan (1988)	PSID 1968–82	Daughters 17–26 in 1982	Received welfare at age t if not receiving at t-1	Family ever received welfare; no. years received welfare	Logit	(+), Sig. effects
Antel (1988a)	NLSY 1979–86	Daughters 14–18 and at home in 1979	Had a birth by age 21; had a premarital birth by age 21	Family on AFDC in 1978	ML adj. for endogeneity of family AFDC receipt	(+), Sig. effects
Antel (1988b)	NLSY 1979–86	Daughters 14–18 and at home in 1979	No. months on AFDC in 1985	Family on AFDC in 1978	ML adj. for endogeneity of family AFDC receipt	(-), Sig. effects
Solon et al. (1988)	PSID 1968–83	Sisters 12–17 in 1968 who were heads and spouses in 1983	Ever received welfare between time sisters left home and 1983	Family ever received welfare between 1968 and time sisters left home	Cross-tabulations	Sister's receipt prob. 22 percentage points higher if from welfare family
Corcoran (1989)	PSID 1968–1983	Male children 25–37 in 1983 who were heads of household	Various measures of income	Family and community background variables	OLS	(-) income returns to low income families and communities. No parental education/overall community effect

TABLE 15 (Continued)

Study	Data set	Population	Dependent variable	Independent variable	Estimating technique	Results
Hill-Ponza (1989)	PSID 1968–85	Women 11–15 living at home	Five measures of welfare dependence when 20–24	Same five measures for family when daughters were 11–15	Probit, Tobit	All effects (+) but strongest on prob. of receiving any welfare at all
Gottschalk (1990a)	NLSY 1979–85	Daughters 14–22 in 1979 living at home	Had a birth at age t if none by t-1; went on AFDC after birth	Family received welfare when daughter at home; proportion at time received	Logit	Mixed pattern of coeeficients; overall (+) effect
Solon et al. (1991)	PSID 1975–1982	Brothers	Annual earnings of brothers	Family background, price inflation, cohort effects	OLS, analysis of variance	Strong (+) family result
Solon (1992)	PSID 1968–1985	Sons 9–17 in 1968 who reported (+) annual income in 1984	Sons earnings	Fathers earnings, age of father and sons	OLS, IV	Large intergenerational income effect
Gottschalk (1992)	PSID 1968–1985	Daughters 18–31 in 1985	AFDC participation; prob. of having a child early	Mothers prior and future AFDC participation, background variables	Jointly estimated duration models, Multinomial logit	Causal link between generations in AFDC participation and birth rates.

TABLE 15 (Continued)

Study	Data set	Population	Dependent variable	Independent variable	Estimating technique	Results
Zimmerman and Levine (1993)	NLS, NLSY 1968–1989	Daughters 14–24 living with parents in 1968	AFDC participation	Mothers AFDC participation, parent's family income, family and daughter background variables.	Bivariate normal probability dist., Reduced form probit model	Little to no real effect of AFDC participation after controlling for income

Notes:
[1] Source: Moffitt, (1992)
[2] Acronyms: PSID = Panel Study of Income Dynamics; NLS= National Longitudinal Survey; NLSY = National Longitudinal Survey of Youth.

marized in Table 15.[30] For example, Gottschalk (1990) shows that the intergenerational correlation holds up when the sample is restricted to include only mothers who were eligible for AFDC, a restriction that eliminates some of the observable and unobservable differences in the family backgrounds of AFDC and non-AFDC mothers. He defines mothers as AFDC recipients if they ever received AFDC, and daughters as AFDC recipients if they received AFDC in one survey year. He finds that 29% of the daughters of AFDC participants received AFDC themselves compared to 12% of the daughters of non-recipient mothers who were eligible.

It is possible that a mother's participation in AFDC itself alters the child's likelihood of AFDC participation. Gottschalk (1990) suggests that models of job matching might explain this kind of causal link. In these models, first time job seekers have imperfect information about possible jobs and it is costly to gather information. If we think of AFDC participation as a 'job', then daughters of AFDC mothers will have much better information about this job than about alternative options. Hence they will be more likely to participate in AFDC rather than engaging in a costly search for alternatives. As Gottschalk puts it 'just as the children of lawyers are more likely to become lawyers, the children of welfare participants are more likely to become participants because the cost of information is lower'. This matching model of intergenerational transmission has not yet been put to an empirical test.

However, if this job-matching hypothesis is correct then AFDC participation should have a much smaller impact on sons than on daughters, since AFDC is not an option for sons. Only one published study examines the effect of maternal AFDC participation on sons. Lerman (1986) finds a significant negative effect of maternal AFDC participation on the earnings of African-American sons in OLS models. This correlation disappears when AFDC participation is instrumented using maternal background variables such as age and education. However, since it is not clear that these variables can legitimately be excluded from the son's earnings equations, these results cannot be considered definitive.

The fact that an intergenerational correlation exists does not establish any causal link between a mother's receipt of AFDC and her daughter's. If

---

[30] Similarly, as Ashenfelter (1983), and Plant (1984) observe, since a persons income is highly correlated over time, it is not surprising that an individual who received welfare last period is more likely to receive welfare this period. This kind of pattern does not, by itself, imply that individuals who receive welfare are likely to become dependent on it.

low maternal income makes it more difficult to provide the education and upbringing that would enable a child to break out of poverty, then the daughter of a poor woman is more likely to be eligible for AFDC than the daughter of a wealthy one. If this is the mechanism underlying the observed inter-generational correlation, then restricting access to AFDC on benefits may only worsen the prospects for poor children.

Zimmerman and Levine (1993) test this hypothesis using data from the original National Longitudinal Surveys and the National Longitudinal Survey of Youth. They regress the daughter's participation in AFDC on measures of maternal participation, maternal income, and other background variables, and find that when income and other background variables are not included in the regression, the correlation between a mother and daughter's probabilities of participation is .16. This correlation falls to .06 when income and background variables are included.

Since both maternal AFDC participation and income may be measured with error, they propose the following instrumental variables technique: instrument AFDC participation using maximum benefit levels in each state, and instrument income using the Duncan index of the mother and father's occupations. The Duncan index is a linear combination of the median earnings and education associated with an individual's occupation. In this equation, maternal AFDC participation has no statistically significant effect on the daughter's probability of participating, once maternal income in controlled for. In summary, these estimates suggest that between 60 and 100% of the observed intergenerational correlation in AFDC participation can be accounted for by intergenerational correlations in income.

C. AFDC Effects on Teen Pregnancy and Childbearing

Several researchers have examined the direct effects of the AFDC program on out-of-wedlock pregnancy among teens. Although the teen birthrate has fallen over time (from 90 births per 1000 in 1955 to 54 per 1000 in 1988), out-of-wedlock births to teenagers have been increasing. Between 1955 and 1988, the rate more than doubled from 15.1 to 37 per 1000 women aged 15 to 19 (US DHHS, various years). Rates of out-of-wedlock teen childbearing are higher for African-Americans than for other groups: in 1985 they accounted for almost a quarter of all births to African-American women. These figures are alarming because out-of-wedlock childbearing by teen mothers is associated with high levels of welfare dependency and poverty (Hofferth and Hayes, 1987) and puts children at risk of physical and developmental delays (Brooks-Gunn and Furstenberg, 1986).

Concern is often expressed that AFDC has contributed to the problem by undermining family values – by supporting single parenthood and allowing teenagers to set up housekeeping on their own once they have a child. The Family Support Act of 1988 eliminated some of the perverse incentives of the system by requiring all states to establish AFDC-UP programs, and to make more strenuous efforts to establish paternity and extract child-support payments from fathers. Still, the fact that pregnancy rates have increased while benefits have decreased suggests that there is no simple relationship between the two.

Moore and Caldwell (1977) were unable to find any consistent effect of state benefit levels or AFDC application acceptance rates on the probability of a teen pregnancy.[31] Their sample consisted of 1,479 African-American and 3,132 other women 15 to 19. Lundberg and Plotnick (1990) report similar results for white teenagers in the NLSY. They do not examine African-American teenagers because of severe under-reporting problems.

Studies of the effects of AFDC on the resolution of pregnancy include Ellwood and Bane (1985), Leibowitz *et al*, (1986), Plotnick (1990), and Duncan and Hoffman (1990). The Ellwood and Bane and Plotnick studies rely on inter-state variation in benefit levels to indentify the effect of AFDC. The only significant effect reported by Ellwood and Bane is on births to never-married women aged 25 to 34. Since these women would be likely to have had children if they were married, Ellwood and Bane interpret these findings as evidence that AFDC affects marital but not fertility behavior.[32] Similarly, Plotnick finds no consistent effect of AFDC on teen child-bearing. The paper by Leibowitz *et al*. focuses on teenagers in Ventura County, California who visited a specific clinic in the first trimester of their pregnancies. They found that girls who were already covered by AFDC (or Medicaid) were significantly less likely to obtain abortions.[33] Moore and Caldwell also found this relationship.

---

[31] However they did find that the availability of family planning clinics had a significant negative effect on the probability of pregnancy.

[32] In their book, Garfinkel and McLanahan (1986) hypothesized that this might be the case.

[33] Lundberg and Plotnick do not find an effect of AFDC benefit levels on the probability of abortion. It may be that familiarity with the system or absence of stigma are more important than generosity.

Duncan and Hoffman point out that all of the previous studies may suffer from an omitted variables bias since they do not take account of a woman's alternative opportunities. Using a sample of African-American teenagers from the Panel Study of Income Dynamics, they construct a measure of opportunities by using the family income of women with similar backgrounds who did not have a teenage birth linked to the receipt of AFDC. They find that AFDC benefits have little effect on the probability of a birth when opportunities are controlled for. In contrast, their measure of economic opportunity has a significant negative effect on the probability of a birth. The authors estimate that if African-American women received the same labor market returns to their characteristics as white women, the incidence of out-of-wedlock teen births would drop 20%. These results should be taken with a grain of salt however, since the authors are in effect constructing their own 'control' group, a process which (as discussed in Chapter 1) can create large biases.

D. Summary

The results reviewed in this chapter suggest that cash income from AFDC has much the same effect on children as cash income from any other source. Whether the cup appears to be half empty or half full depends on one's perspective. There is no evidence that AFDC participation *per se* is harmful to children. But there is also no evidence that the benefits of public expenditures on AFDC accrue mainly to children. Still, the limited number of studies and small range of outcomes that have been examined suggest that further research is necessary before firm conclusions can be drawn.

5. MEDICAID

As we saw in Chapter 3, spending on children under the Medicaid program constitutes one of the largest in-kind transfers to children and exceeds the amount spent on AFDC. The introduction of Medicaid in 1966 coincided with decreases in infant mortality, increases in hospitalization rates for poor children, and an increase in the frequency of doctor visits for poor children relative to non-poor children (Danzinger and Stern, 1990; Starfield, 1985; Colle and Grossman, 1978). Hence, Medicaid seems to have played an important role in reducing inequities in the utilization of health care.

Despite these advances, America's children appear to be in poor health relative to those in other industrial countries. In addition to the high infant mortality rates discussed above, US children under 15 years of age had 28% more disability days and 44 percent more bed days than Canadian children. US children under 1 year of age had a 14% higher mortality rate and those 1 to 4 years of age had a mortality rate 8% higher than Canadian children (Kozak and McCarthy, 1984). These high rates of morbidity and mortality suggest that poor children in the United States are receiving an inadequate quantity or quality of health care, relative to children in other countries.

Inadequate care could reflect the fact that until recently, many poor children were not covered by Medicaid. If the problem were one of coverage alone, then the recent extension of Medicaid coverage to all poor children should have a dramatic effect on children's health. Alternatively, Medicaid coverage may be of lower quality than private insurance coverage, or the poor may face obstacles to care that cannot be addressed simply by expanding coverage.

Finally, the link between the utilization of care and health status is not at all clear. It is possible for example, that, because of interactions between a person's environment and the effectiveness of medical care, a poor child requires more medical intervention than a rich one to achieve the same health status. This chapter focuses on the utilization of care by Medicaid-eligible children and closes with a discussion of the link between the utilization of care and child health.

A. Insurance Coverage and Utilization of Care

The uninsured are known to receive less health care than the insured (Davis and Reynolds, 1976; Manning et al., 1987). And in 1988, 17% of all children and 28% of children with family incomes less than $10,000 were without health insurance coverage of any kind (Bloom, 1990). Seventeen percent of children without health insurance do not have a regular provider of pediatric care compared to 5% of privately insured children (Butler et al., 1985).

However, it is possible that even children covered by the Medicaid program are inadequately served. Less than half of Medicaid eligible children born in the district of Columbia get all their shots, despite the fact that mothers receive written reminders (*The Washington Post*, 1993). One reason may be a lack of providers: Butler et al. (1985) report that 10% of Medicaid-covered children lack a regular source of care. Sloan, Mitchell and Cromwell (1978) and Decker (1993) find that many doctors do not participate in the Medicaid program and Decker also finds that those who do serve Medicaid patients spend significantly less time with their patients than other doctors. Yudkowsky *et al.* (1992) reports that the number of pediatricians willing to accept Medicaid patients declined from 85% in 1978 to 77% in 1989 and that the proportion of pediatricians who limited the number of Medicaid patients in their practices increased from 26% to 39% over the decade. One reason for low participation rates may be that Medicaid fees are on average 75% of a doctor's usual fee.[34]

Many states limit the services available to Medicaid patients: for instance in fiscal year 1986, Texas did not cover clinic services, Connecticut did not cover emergency services and New Hampshire restricted Medicaid patients to 12 outpatient visits per year (US Health Care Financing Administration, 1988). Finally, bureaucratic delays may pose a significant barrier to timely care: for example, the average delay in processing applications is 4 weeks (AGI, 1988).

i) The Effects of Medicaid

Currie and Thomas (1993a) use the 86 and 88 waves of the National Longitudinal Survey's Child Mother file to examine the relationship between insurance coverage and the health care utilization of older children. In each year, mothers were asked whether their child's health care was covered by either Medicaid or by private insurance. The ability to distinguish between Medicaid and private insurance is useful because children with private insurance coverage tend to be better off in observable (and presumably also in unobservable) dimensions than children with Medicaid coverage. Hence, if the two types of coverage are found to have similar effects, then the effects

---

[34] According to a survey conducted by the Alan Guttmacher Institute in 1986, there are many other reasons why doctors do not participate in the program. In their words: 'There is more red tape under Medicaid than under private insurance. Medicaid often uses a different claim form from other insurers, requiring a separate computer system; it sometimes uses different procedure codes or diagnosis codes on its claim forms; claims are paid late and are sometimes denied on a technicality; in some states Medicaid funds are exhausted part way through the year and no further claims are paid; there are often different rules and reimbursement schedules for clinics, hospitals and physicians, complicating the practice of physicians who work in more than one setting; reimbursement policies change frequently but providers are often not notified of the changes until after claims have already been denied...' etc. (AGI, 1988).

are likely to reflect insurance coverage rather than omitted characteristics correlated with selection into either Medicaid or private insurance programs. The measures of health care analyzed are (1) whether or not the child had

TABLE 16

OLS Estimates of the Effect of Medicaid and Private
Insurance on the Health Care of Older Children

	Routine Checkup			Visits for illness		
	(1)	*(2)*	*(3)*	*(4)*	*(5)*	*(6)*
Age in 88:	1-2	3-4	5-9	1-2	3-4	5-9
Intercept	.016	.755	.110	-1.997	-.245	-.109
	(.299)	(.345)	(.287)	(2.014)	(1.266)	(.964)
African-American	0.339	-.662	.453	-3.434	-.560	-.559
	(.512)	(.581)	(.449)	(3.447)	(2.126)	(1.508)
Type of Insurance						
Medicaid	.087	.132	.090	.424	.350	.215
	(.038)	(.040)	(.031)	(.254)	(.146)	(.105)
African-American	-.025	-.016	.065	-.531	-.261	-.149
* Medicaid	(.065)	(.069)	(.051)	(.439)	(.254)	(.172)
Private Ins.	.023	.042	.042	.468	.214	.220
	(.029)	(.026)	(.026)	(.198)	(.122)	(.089)
African-American	-.007	.043	.020	-.669	.006	-.186
* Privat Ins.	(.057)	(.64)	(.047)	(.386)	(.232)	(.159)
Maternal Characteristics						
Permanent Income	.016	-.033	-.018	.193	.074	.059
	(.028)	(.033)	(.028)	(.192)	(.119)	(.093)
African-American	-.032	-.078	-.049	.342	.010	.021
* Income	(.050)	(.056)	(.044)	(.337)	(.204)	(.148)
Top Grade in 88	.016	.014	.001	.113	.073	.058
	(.006)	(.007)	(.006)	(.040)	(.027)	(.020)
African-American	-.017	-.008	.030	-.001	-.038	-.021
* Top Grade	(.031)	(.015)	(.011)	(.087)	(.055)	(.037)
R-Squared	.045	.058	.036	.052	.040	.031
# Observations	2111	2192	3674	2111	2192	3674

Notes:

Standard errors in parentheses. All regressions also included: the mother's AFQT score; an indicator equal to 1 if she lived in an urban area at age 14; the child's gender; county income per capita; the number of physicians per 1000 state residents; the number of hospital beds per 1000 state residents; the state infant mortality rates; dummy variables for residence in the northeast, south, or west; and interactions of all these variables with the indicator for African-Americans. Since observations from both the 1986 and 1988 NLSCM surveys have been pooled, a control for the earlier survey was included to allow for possible differences between the two waves.

Source: Currie and Thomas (1993a).

a routine health checkup in the past 6 months[35], and (2) the number of ill-nesses requiring medical attention in the past year. As discussed in Chapter 2, the number of illnesses confounds morbidity with the utilization of medical care. However, since the number of visits increases with maternal income and education, it appears to be a measure of the propensity to utilize care as well as of morbidity.

Ordinary Least Squares estimates of the probability that a child had a routine health checkup in the past 6 months and of the number of illnesses requiring medical attention in the past year are shown in Table 16. These regressions include dummy variables for both Medicaid coverage and private health insurance coverage. The excluded category is no insurance. The models also include a full set of interactions with an indicator equal to one if the child is African-American. This specification is equivalent to estimating separate models for whites and African-Americans, but allows a ready comparison of the effects of insurance coverage on the two groups. The complete set of control variables is listed in the table notes.

The linear probability models for doctor checkups show that Medicaid coverage is estimated to increase the probability of a routine checkup by between 6% and 16%, depending on age and race. There are no statistically significant effects of private health insurance coverage on the probability of a routine checkup. This result may reflect the fact that many private insurance policies do not cover pediatric preventive care (Mitchell and Schurman, 1984), so that children do not receive regular preventive care until they enter the school system.

Turning to the number of illnesses requiring medical attention, white children with either Medicaid coverage or private insurance receive more visits for illness than those without insurance coverage. White children 1 to 2 years old receive half a visit more than children who have no coverage, but the benefits of both private insurance and Medicaid tend to fall with age. In contrast, neither Medicaid coverage nor private insurance coverage has any significant effect on the number of doctor visits for African-Americans.

The OLS models discussed above do not control for selection into the program. It is possible to do better using these data, because, in many cases, there are repeated measures of the same child. Hence, it is possible to examine *changes* in health care utilization between 1986 and 1988 and relate them to *changes* in the child's health insurance status. As discussed in Chapter

---

[35] Respondents were actually asked to choose one of seven categories. Categories 1 to 3 and categories 4 to 7 were grouped together to obtain the 6 month cutoff.

2, this procedure controls for any fixed unobserved characteristics such as
the child's innate healthiness. Currie and Thomas (1993a) show that in this
example, fixed effects estimates are remarkably similar to those obtained
by OLS.

In summary, children with Medicaid coverage are more likely to have
routine checkups than children with either private health insurance coverage or no insurance coverage. Among white children, both kinds of insurance coverage increase the number of doctor's visits for illness, but neither
Medicaid nor private insurance coverage have any effect on the number of
visits for illness among African-American children.

These results are remarkably similar to those obtained by Colle and
Grossman (1978) using OLS on a 1970 cross-section: they found that Medicaid coverage was associated with a higher probability of a doctor's visit in
the past 12 months, but that private insurance coverage had little effect on
the probability of receiving preventive care. Decker (1993) has also repli-
cated the results regarding the differential effects of insurance coverage on
the number of doctor visits for illness among white and African-American
children using a recent cross-section of data from the National Medical Care
Expenditure Survey.[36]

ii) Explaining Racial Differences In Patterns of Utilization

The racial difference in the number of visits for illness among children with
insurance coverage is difficult to explain. It is unlikely to be generated purely
by differences in the way that whites and African-Americans are selected
into the program. First, the fact that the OLS and fixed effects results are
very similar suggests that once observable characteristics such as income
and education are controlled for, biases associated with fixed omitted unobserved variables are not very important. Second, Medicaid coverage increases
the probability of a routine checkup among both African-Americans and
whites. If what we were seeing was an artifact of selection into the Medicaid program, then we might expect similar racial patterns in the models for
checkups and in the models for the number of visits for illness. Finally,
private insurance coverage and Medicaid coverage have very similar effects on the number of visits for illness, although one would expect selection into private insurance to be governed by a different mechanism than
selection into Medicaid.

---

[36] Rosenbach (1989) reports a similar result using the 1980 National Medical Care Utilization and Expenditure Survey.

A second hypothesis is that African-American children tend to live in areas that are under-served, so that it is difficult for them to get additional visits for illness. Residential segregation may play an important role in determining the access of African-American children to medical services. For example, Fossett *et al.* (1993) report that in Chicago in 1987, there were twice as many children per office-based pediatrician in the inner city compared to the best served neighborhoods, and 60% more children per child health care provider. And Adams (1992) reports that inner-city residents remained under-served even after generous increases in Medicaid reimbursements.

In addition, African-American children are twice as likely as white children to receive care in an 'organised setting' such as a clinic or emergency room rather than a private provider, HMO, or prepaid group practice (Bloom, 1990). There is also some evidence that the number of providers serving low income children declined during the 1980s (Perloff, 1992). In this case, the elimination of racial differences in the utilization of care depends on improving the provision of services to these communities. However, to be completely consistent with Currie and Thomas' results, it would have to be the case that barriers to obtaining checkups were smaller than barriers associated with obtaining additional visits for illness.

It is quite conceivable that barriers to some forms of care are higher than barriers to others. St. Peter *et al.* (1992) find that although Medicaid children are more likely than poor children without Medicaid to have a regular source of care, compared to children above the poverty line, Medicaid children are more likely to have different usual sources of care for routine care and for sick care. In particular, they are more likely to use an emergency department as their regular source of sick care.

A third possibility is that African-American and white parents have different attitudes about the optimal number of visits for illness, perhaps because African-American mothers are more likely to be employed and/or single parents so that it may be more costly for them to take a child to the doctor for repeated visits. In any case, these results suggest that while Medicaid coverage increases the utilization of preventive care, it does not eliminate racial differences in patterns of utilization.

iii) The Effects of Medicaid Expansions

As discussed in Chapter 3, the Federal government began expanding the Medicaid coverage of pregnant women and children beginning in 1984. By January 1992, a uniform, minimum floor for coverage had been established that was 2 to 3 times higher than the floor that had existed in the average state only 4 years earlier. It is estimated that when these expansions are fully phased in, the number of uninsured children will fall by 39% (Marquis and Long, 1992).

In addition, most states have overhauled the administration of Medicaid services for pregnant women with the aim of improving access. As of January 1992, 48 states had dropped asset tests that prevented some women from gaining Medicaid eligibility, 26 had adopted 'presumptive eligibility' – rules that presume that a pregnant applicant will qualify while processing her claim, and 33 had shortened their application forms (National Governor's Association, 1992). Several states have also adopted public relation campaigns with themes such as 'Baby Your Baby' (Utah) or 'Baby Love' (North Carolina) with the aim of drawing women into care (NGA, 1992).

Similar efforts aimed at increasing the enrollment rates of eligible children are still at a very early stage (NGA, 1992). Rymer and Adler (1987) report that many low-income families and their physicians are unaware that they can qualify for Medicaid even if they do not receive AFDC benefits. Non-AFDC children who do become enrolled due to a medical crisis, tend to be enrolled for shorter periods than AFDC children. It seems that once their need for acute care is met, they are likely to leave the rolls.

It seems appropriate then to focus on studies of the effects that Medicaid expansions have had on the utilization of prenatal care. Piper *et al.* (1990) discuss the expansion of Medicaid benefits to all married women who met AFDC income cutoffs in Tennessee in 1985. The study examines Medicaid enrollment rates, the utilization of prenatal care, and birthweights in the years before and after the change. Medicaid enrollment rates rose in all maternal groups with the largest increase among married women younger than 25 who had less than a high school education. For whites in this group, enrollment rose from 24% to 42%, while for African-Americans, it rose from 32% to 53%. There was no similar increase among single women, so the extension of coverage seems to have been effectively translated into an increase in enrollments.

On the other hand, there was a significant increase in the proportion of women who delayed obtaining prenatal care past the first trimester. Among the group with the largest absolute increase in enrollments (married white women less than 25 without a highschool education), the proportion of women who enrolled in Medicaid during the 30 days prior to delivery jumped from 12% to 29%. It is likely that many of these women were actually enrolled when they arrived at the hospital to give birth.

An evaluation of the North Carolina Baby Love program produced dramatically different results. As required by law, North Carolina extended Medicaid eligibility to pregnant women with incomes less than 100% of the Federal poverty line in 1988. The old threshold was about 40% of the poverty line. In addition, the state introduced 'maternity care coordinators'. These coordinators visit each pregnant woman at least once a month. They encourage healthy behavior and provide assistance by linking the woman up with other social services such as housing assistance and WIC.

Buescher *et al.* (1991) compare the prenatal care and neo-natal outcomes of the 15,526 Medicaid-eligible women who received coordination services in 1988 and 1989 to those of the 34,463 Medicaid-eligible women who did not.[37] Hence, their evaluation focuses on the Baby Love program rather than on the accompanying expansion of Medicaid eligibility.

They find that women who received coordination services had characteristics that suggest that they were at slightly higher risk of having a low birth weight baby than those who did not: they were more likely to be African-American, unmarried, less than 18, and have less than 12 years of education. But the authors find that rates of WIC participation were 91% in the group that received coordination services compared to 67% in the group that did not. The rate of low birth weight was 8.7% among the women who received care coordination compared to 10.5% among those who did not. And infant mortality rates among the two groups were 9.9 and 12.2 per 1,000, respectively.

These results must, however, be interpreted with caution due to two possible sources of selection bias. First, many providers did not offer the Baby Love program, and little information is available about the differences between providers who did and did not offer it. Secondly, provided a program was available, women could choose whether or not to be enrolled. Women who were enrolled were more likely to obtain postpartum examinations and to obtain Well-Baby care for their babies. These differences could reflect either the lasting effects of the program or the fact that these mothers were more motivated than others.

Currie and Gruber (1993) use national samples from Vital Statistics, the Current Population Survey and the National Longitudinal Survey's Child Mother file to examine the impact of Medicaid expansions on the usage of prenatal care, the incidence of low birthweight, and infant mortality. Using

---

[37] Women who received no prenatal care were excluded from the sample.

CPS data, they first construct two measures of the generosity of state Medicaid programs in each year. The first is the fraction of women aged 15 to 44 who would have been eligible for Medicaid had they become pregnant. The second measure controls for non-programmatic sources of heterogeneity between states by drawing a random sample of US women in each year and calculating the percentage of them who would have been eligible under each state's rules. Using this second measure, Currie and Gruber find evidence that the 20% increase in the fraction of women eligible for Medicaid in the event of pregnancy which occurred over the 80s was associated with a 2% decrease in the incidence of low birthweight, and a 7% decrease in the infant mortality rate.[38]

However, they find that the early expansions of Medicaid coverage to poor women who had been ineligible for AFDC for reasons of family structure (e.g. single pregnant women without eligible children) had much greater effects on infant health than later extensions of coverage to women with incomes between 100% and 185% of the poverty line. Their analysis of self-reported Medicaid coverage in the CPS, and of data on Medicaid expenditures suggests that many women in the latter group did not take up their new benefits.

The evidence from the Medicaid expansions is consistent with previous findings that while they have a positive effect, extensions of insurance eligibility alone do not eliminate inequities in the utilization of health care. For example, the Rand Health Insurance Experiment found that among infants with free care, only 60% received timely immunizations for DPT and polio compared to 45% of infants in the sample as a whole (Lurie, 1987).

B. The Link Between Utilization of Medical Care and Child Health

With the exception of the analysis of effects on birthweight, the discussion above emphasizes the effects of Medicaid coverage on the utilization of medical care rather than on health *per se*. The reason is that utilization is both easier to measure, and perhaps more directly influenced by public policy than health itself. There are many medical services whose effects on health are unknown. It is for example, difficult to translate the additional half-visit for illness among white children discussed above into a statement about

---

[38] In her study of the adoption of the Canadian health insurance system, Hanratty (1992) also finds a bigger effect on infant mortality rates than on the incidence of low birthweight.

health, given that the efficacy of treatments for many common childhood illnesses has not been demonstrated (Starfield, 1985).

It is also difficult to assess the benefits of visits for preventive care. The majority of pediatric visits are for well care and include immunizations, physical exams, and parental guidance. While immunizations are extremely important, a substantial literature shows that few physical abnormalities are detected during routine well-child physicals, (US Congress, Office of Technology Assessment, 1988) and that on average physicians spend less than 1.5 minutes per visit with parents of young children (Reisinger and Bires (1980)).

Even if we knew what forms of care were most effective, it is unlikely that equalizing access to these forms of care would eliminate differences in health status. Poor children suffer from 'double jeopardy' in that their circumstances not only make them more likely to suffer prematurity, poor nutrition, illness, and accidents, but also make it harder for them to recover from these shocks (Wise, 1988).

C. Summary

The evidence reviewed in this chapter suggests that the utilization of care and some health outcomes may be improved by expanding the health insurance coverage of poor children. However, significant race and income differentials in health status are likely to remain. Current state-level experiments with the Medicaid program suggest that these differentials may be reduced through innovative programs to increase the enrollment of eligibles. But the health consequences of poverty are unlikely to be entirely eliminated by public health insurance programs.

6. THE FOOD STAMP PROGRAM

Analyses of the Food Stamp Program (FSP) have focused on two questions: first, is there evidence that children in Food Stamp households are better nourished than those in non-participant households? And second, is the household's propensity to buy food out of Food Stamp income any higher than its propensity to buy food out of cash income? This second question has a bearing on whether the additional administrative costs of an in-kind transfer program can be justified. This chapter reviews the available evidence.

TABLE 17
Household Nutrient Availability as a Percentage
of the RDA for Persons Eating in the Households

Nutrient	FSP Participants (a)	FSP Nonparticipants (b)	Difference (a-b)
Food Energy	139%	121%	+18%
Protein	232	203	+29
Calcium	119	111	+8
Iron	151	137	+14
Magnesium	134	123	+11
Phosphorous	202	183	+19
Vitamin A	213	178	+35
Thiamin	194	165	+29
Riboflavin	204	180	+24
Vitamin B6	132	114	+18
Vitamin B12	235	191	+44
Vitamin C	290	264	+26

Notes:
The table shows mean nutrient availability per equivalent nutrition unit as a percentage of the RDA. Household size in ENU's is a measure of size that adjusts for the age and sex composition of household members, the number of meals per week that they eat from the household food supply, and meals served to guests.

This table is from Fraker, T., The Effects of Food Stamps on Food Consumption: A Review of the Literature, Current Perspectives on Food Stamp Participation, USDA, 1990.

A. Effects on Nutrition

i) Nutrient Availability

Much of the available evidence about the nutritional effects of the Food Stamp Program is indirect in the sense that it measures the effects of food stamp receipt on the money value of food used by households, or on the 'availability' of nutrients in the food purchased for home consumption. Table 17 shows a comparison of household nutrient availabilities for Food Stamp participants and for non-participant households. Food Stamp participants have uniformly higher household nutrient availabilities than non-participants. These nutrient availabilities are measured relative to the US Recommended Daily Allowance (RDA) for the family. Fraker (1990a) reviews 8 studies of household nutrient availabilities that show that differences between Food Stamp participants and non-participants remain when other

TABLE 18
Nutrient Intake as a Percentage of the RDA:
Mean Per Individual, One Day of Intake Data

Nutrient	FSP Participants (a)	FSP Nonparticipants (b)	Difference (a-b)
Food Energy	85%	83%	+2%
Protein	172	168	+4
Calcium	87	90	-3
Iron	96	100	-4
Magnesium	85	88	-3
Phosphorous	130	132	-2
Vitamin A	132	118	+14
Thiamin	130	113	+17
Riboflavin	141	132	+9
Vitamin B6	79	72	+7
Vitamin B12	142	143	-1
Vitamin C	144	133	+11

Notes:
This table is from Fraker, T., The Effects of Food Stamps on Food Consumption: A Review of the Literature, Current Perspectives on Food Stamp Participation, USDA, 1990.

observable differences between the households are controlled for using multivariate techniques.[39]

Three of these studies, Allen and Gadson (1983), Basiotis et al. (1983), and Devaney, Haines, and Moffitt (1989) focus on the availability of these nutrients whose deficiency in US diets is of special concern: Vitamin C, calcium, and iron. All three studies suggest that participation in the Food Stamp Program increases the availability of these nutrients. However, the Devaney, Haines and Moffitt study is the only one that controls for possible unobserved differences between Food Stamp participants and non-participants. They report that the effects of selection into the program are not significant, but do not give details about how they were estimated.

A related study by Kisker and Devaney (1988) compares the food purchases of low-income households that meet the US RDAs to the purchases of households that do not. It documents relatively small differences in consumption patterns. For example, households that meet the RDAs purchase greater proportions of fresh fruits and vegetables. However, these households differ from households that fall short of the RDAs mainly because

---

[39] Most studies of the Food Stamp Program are based on the Nationwide Food Consumption Surveys of the USDA, the Bureau of Labor Statistics Consumer Expenditure Survey, and the Panel Study of Income Dynamics. These data sets are described in the Data Appendix.

they consume greater quantities of all foods, rather than because they consume more nutritious types of food. This comparison suggests that while it is possible that households that do not meet the US RDA make poor food choices, their choices are no worse on average than those of other low-income households. Hence, the capacity to improve RDAs by altering the composition of people's consumption baskets may be rather limited.

ii) Individual Nutrient Intakes

Table 18 gives a comparison of the individual nutrient intakes of Food Stamp participants and non-participants. In contrast to measures of household nutrient availability, these measures usually include both food consumed at home and food consumed away from home. Table 18 suggests that the FSP has no effect on individual nutrient intakes, a result that is surprising in light of the positive effects on nutrient availability at the household level. Once again, Fraker's (1990a) survey suggests that this result holds up in a multivariate context.

Studies that focus specifically on the nutrient intakes of children include Rush et al. (1986), Fraker, Long, and Post (1990), and Fraker (1990b). The last study finds a positive effect of Food Stamp participation on 7 of 16 nutrients examined using OLS regressions. The author goes on to correct the estimates for selection into the program using maximum FSP benefits as one of the instrumental variables. This correction increases standard errors without altering coefficient estimates, which suggests that positive and significant effects of the FSP might conceivably be found in larger samples.

The results of Korenman and Miller (1992) are also inconclusive. They use data from the National Longitudinal Survey of Youth to examine the effect of FSP participation during pregnancy on birthweight, the incidence of low birthweight, gestational age, the incidence of prematurity, and on the mother's weight gain during pregnancy. In OLS regressions, they find a statistically significant effect of participation by women with incomes less than 50% of the poverty line on the birthweights of first-born children. However, they find no effects for children of higher birth order, or when they control for unobserved characteristics of the mother using fixed effects models. They also report that the height-for-age of children whose families received food stamps in the year prior to the survey is significantly *lower* than that of other children, which highlights the importance of controlling for unobserved heterogeneity when evaluating the efficacy of social programs.

iii) Reconciling Studies of Household Nutrient Availability with Studies of Individual Intakes

Fraker (1990b) argues that the sample sizes needed to detect the effects of the FSP on individual nutrient intakes probably exceed the sample sizes needed to detect effects on household nutrient availability because measures of individual nutrient intakes are typically collected over a fairly short time period such as a day. Since the day-to-day variability in a person's food intake can be quite large, estimates of individual nutrient intake may be less precise than estimates of household food availability that are based on food diaries kept over several days or even weeks.

Alternatively, the differences may be an artifact of various adjustments that are often made to household-level data. Food Stamp households differ from non-participant households in several ways: they are more likely to be female-headed, have more children, and consume less food away from home. Studies that examine the nutrient availability of food consumed at home typically adjust consumption to account for differences in household composition using equivalence scales. These scales weight each person in the household using the average nutritional needs of a person of that gender and age group relative to an adult male.

Suppose, for example, that the equivalence scale simply assumes that the RDA of an adult woman is 75% of the RDA for an adult man rather than adjusting for the compositional differences in men and women's dietary needs. Then if the man and woman consume the same amount of a given nutrient, the woman will be more likely to have consumed 100% of the RDA just because the target amount to be consumed is lower. Including household demographic information in the regression model would provide a simple test of the adequacy of the equivalence scale – if adjustment using the equivalence scale works, then demographic variables will not be statistically significant.[40]

Adjustments to household nutrient availability are also made to account for the proportion of food consumed away from home. Inaccuracies in these

---

[40] See Deaton and Muellbauer (1986) for a recent discussion of the problems involved in the construction of equivalence scales. A less restrictive way to allow for household composition would be to include the number of persons in each age-gender category as independent variables. A further advantage of this specification is that these variables can be interacted with the measure of Food Stamp Program benefits, so that the marginal propensity to consume out of Food Stamp income is allowed to vary with household composition (see Chavas and Yeung, 1982).

adjustments could lead to biased estimates of FSP effects. For example, if the nutritional content of meals away from home is assumed to be too low, the Food Stamp households will be more likely to meet their combined RDAs simply because they are less likely to eat away from home. The fact that the FSP seems to have very little effect on individual nutrient intakes may indicate that the treatment of meals away from home is of crucial importance.

B. Effects on Food Expenditures

i) Marginal Propensities to Consume Out of FSP and Cash Income

If a household's FSP benefits exceeded the amount that the household wished to spend on food (and there was no market in 'surplus' stamps), then we would expect households to consume the entire amount of their FSP benefit in the form of food. In reality, 85 to 90% of participating households have food expenditures that exceed the value of their FSP benefits. These households can use food stamps to purchase food they would buy in any case, and use the money that is 'freed up' to purchase other commodities. This does not mean that food stamps will have no impact on food expenditures, but it does suggest that a household's marginal propensity of consume out of Food Stamp income should not differ from its marginal propensity to consume out of cash income.

It is surprising then that every study of this question has found that the marginal propensity to consume food out of Food Stamp income is at least twice as high as the marginal propensity to consume food out of cash income. Fraker (1990a) reviews 17 of these studies. The three most recent, Chen (1983), Senauer and Young (1986), and Fraker, Long, and Post (1990), use three different data sets but arrive at very similar estimates. They find that for every dollar of Food Stamp income, $.23 to $.29 is spent on food compared to $.05 to $.11 out of every dollar of cash income.

Several potential explanations of these results have been advanced. First, it has been argued (Fraker, 1990a) that the difference is due to the fact that Food Stamp benefits are paid monthly rather than weekly or bi-weekly as most forms of cash income are. It has been found that Food Stamp households are far more likely than non-participant households to do their major food shopping on a monthly rather than a weekly basis. For example, data from a demonstration project in Reading, PA, found that recipients spent

19% of their monthly FSP benefits on the day of issuance, 70% within the first week, and 89% within the first 2 weeks of issuance (Fraker, 1990a). However, in principle, the timing of payments should not affect the total amount purchased during the month unless households would be so constrained in the absence of the program that they could not purchase some more expensive food items at all.

A second hypothesis is that households view FSP income as more 'permanent' than other relatively more 'transitory' sources of cash income. For example, if members of FSP households tend to hold insecure jobs then they may view employment income as transitory. Households are thought to adjust consumption behavior more in response to permanent changes in their incomes than in response to transitory changes. The hypothesis that the differences in marginal propensities to consume are due to the relative permanence of FSP income could be tested by distinguishing between FSP households with relatively stable and unstable sources of cash income, or by estimating the marginal propensities to consume out of different kinds of cash income.

A third potential explanation is that women with children have higher marginal propensities to purchase food than men and that the female head of household has more control of Food Stamp coupons (which are likely to be issued in her name) than she has over the household's cash income. In other words, the issuance of Food Stamp coupons in the woman's name may increase her bargaining power within the household and allow her to purchase more of goods that she values.

Some evidence consistent with this proposition comes from the Washington State Welfare Reform Demonstration Program (Fraker, 1990). AFDC recipients in demonstration counties had the option of choosing to receive their AFDC and Food Stamp benefits in the form of a single consolidated check rather than continuing to receive Food Stamp coupons. Yet over 20% of these women opted to continue receiving the coupons.

Finally, unobserved differences between participant and non-participant households may be of great importance since historically, only about half of eligible households have participated in the FSP. Studies indicate that the most persistent barrier to participation is lack of information about the program. Many people do not apply because they believe that their incomes are too high, or because they believe that they are ineligible for other reasons. People in the first situation may be unaware that a proportion of earned income will be disregarded in the computation of family income. People in the second situation might believe, for example, that home ownership disqualifies them.

These informational barriers appear to have been of great importance over a long period of time. In 1974, the Department of Agriculture was placed under a court order to increase its efforts to inform eligible households about the program (Coe, 1979). However, using data from 1979, Coe (1983) found that 40% of eligible households in a sample drawn from the Panel Study of Income Dynamics believed that they were ineligible. Surprisingly, this fraction did not vary greatly with the education of the respondent – better educated people were more likely to know about the program, but also more likely to believe that they were ineligible. A recent survey of 2,335 low-income families found that 37% of those eligible for food stamps were not receiving them (Food Research and Action (FRAC), 1991). Seventeen percent of the respondents had never applied for food stamps and of these, 65% said they had not applied because they did not believe that they were eligible.

Stigma associated with using the stamps is another often-mentioned barrier to participation. The stigma associated with using Food Stamps may be greater than the stigma attached to utilization of other welfare programs, since they are highly visible. There have been reports of women on AFDC who do not apply for Food Stamps even though they are automatically eligible and have been informed about the program (*New York Times*, April 20, 1986.) Twenty-one percent of the eligibles in the FRAC survey who said they had not applied for Food Stamps cited stigma as the major reason. Interestingly, Coe (1983) reports that households with more children were less likely to cite stigma as a reason not to apply.

Finally, unobserved characteristics associated with selection into the program are potentially of great importance. If for example, households that know more about nutrition or that place a high value on food expenditures are systematically more likely to enroll in the program, then positive effects of the FSP on household expenditures and nutrient availabilities may reflect nothing more than this selection bias.

ii) Evidence from Food Stamp 'Cashouts'

More direct evidence about the relationship between the marginal propensities to consume out of Food Stamp income and other income comes from the SSI/Elderly Food Stamp Cashout Demonstration (Blanchard *et al.*, 1982); Butler, Ohls, and Posner, 1985) and the Puerto Rico Nutrition Assistance

Program (Beebout *et al.*, 1985; Devaney and Fraker, 1986; Moffitt, 1989). The SSI/Elderly cashout substituted cash for coupons in 4 demonstration counties and compared the outcomes to those in 4 matched comparison counties. In Puerto Rico, the whole system was converted to cash in 1982.

Evaluations of these projects found that the marginal propensities to consume out of Food Stamp and other income were equal. However, in Puerto Rico, where Food Stamp Program benefits were high relative to an average family's food expenditures, an active black market in stamps existed before the cashout, so it is not surprising to find that stamps were treated like cash.

The contrast between the results for the low-income elderly and the results for families with children are more striking. A possible explanation is that in families with children, resources in the hands of mothers are more likely to be spent on food for children than resources in the hands of fathers[41], whereas in elderly households without children the preferences of men and women are more similar.

If correct, this hypothesis would have important implications for welfare reform, and for program evaluation. Economic analyses of the effects of welfare tend to treat the family as a monolith that maximizes its utility by making choices given the constraints it faces (Becker, 1981). If family members have different preferences, then we must consider the way that welfare programs affect bargaining power and resource allocations within the household.

C. Summary

Evaluations of the Food Stamp Program yield three findings. First, participating households have higher nutrient availabilities. Second, individual nutrient intakes are no higher in these households than in non-participating households. And third, among families with children, the marginal propensity to consume food out of food stamp income is double the propensity to buy food out of other cash income.

On the whole, this is a very puzzling set of results. Future research should focus on reconciling the difference between household nutrient availability and individual nutrient intakes. It is conceivable that the results for nutrient

---

[41] There have been few empirical studies of this question in the United States. The fact that only a quarter of absent fathers pay any child support (Corbett, 1993) provides some *primae facie* evidence that men and women have different preferences. Thomas (1992) shows that in the United States, the education of the mother has a greater impact on the height of a child than the education of the father, conditional on income and parental heights.

availabilities are biased by the use of *ad hoc* equibalence scales and adjustments for meals away from home. Studies of nutrient intakes also tend to suffer from smaller sample sizes and higher variances in day-to-day intakes that make it difficult to identify the effects of the program. And both types of studies suffer from selection biases since many people who are eligible for food stamps do not participate.

Finally if it is true that the marginal propensity to consume food out of food stamp income exceeds the marginal propensity to consume out of cash income, then the reasons for this difference should be investigated. One of the most interesting hypotheses is that women exert more control over FSP income than they do over cash income, and that women with children have higher marginal propensities to purchase food than men. If this hypothesis proved true, it would have important implications for the way that welfare benefits to families should be targeted.

7. WIC AND SCHOOL NUTRITION PROGRAMS

Chapter 3 showed that WIC was one of the fastest growing federal welfare programs. Its popularity rests on evaluations of the program that find reductions in infant mortality, rates of low birthweight, and Medicaid costs, and improvements in birthweight, gestational age, and cognitive achievement. WIC is one of the most directly targeted and interventionist of federal welfare programs. Eligibility is often determined by medical examinations and blood tests, and nutritional counselling is required. In addition, the types and even the brands of foods that can be purchased are strictly controlled. Hence, comparisons of WIC with programs such as AFDC raise one of the fundamental questions of welfare reform: can the government trust parents to use income transfers in the way that is best for their children, or must the government assume a more paternalistic role in order to ensure that children benefit? School nutrition programs have not captured the public's attention in the way that WIC has although these programs currently affect many more children.

This chapter reviews evaluations of the WIC and school nutrition programs.[42] Although the evidence is far from conclusive, the available studies suggest that 'WIC Works'[43], and that school nutrition programs can and do

---

[42] The review of the WIC literature is selective. For a more complete list of references see Food Research and Action Center, Jan. 1991.

[43] This is the advertising slogan for the WIC program in Massachusetts.

TABLE 19
Summary of Major WIC Evaluations[1]

Study	Comparison groups	Selected outcomes examined	Summary of reported impacts on the outcomes relevant to WIC/Medicaid Study	Data source
Edozien, Switzer and Bryan (1979)	WIC participants at enrollment (compared with the characteristics of a current WIC participant group)	Birthweight Infant mortality Growth of children Anemia and other measures of nutritional status	Increased birthweight	Over 50,000 women, infants and children in 19 WIC projects in 14 states; clinical examinations and laboratory tests carried out between 1973 and 1976
Kennedy, Gershoff Reed, and Austin (1982)	(1) Pregnant WIC applicants not certified because program had no slots, or those who applied and were certified postpartum (2) Pregnant women at non-WIC health facilities Demographics of pregnant non-WIC participants were matched with the demographics of WIC participants	Birthweight	Increased birthweight (3,273 vs. 3,136 grams) that also increased with the number of WIC food instruments	Medical and nutrition records for 1,297 live births (897 to WIC participants, 400 to non-WIC) and 9 sites in Massachusetts between 1973 and 1978

TABLE 19 (Continued).

Study	Comparison groups	Selected outcomes examined	Summary of reported impacts on the outcomes relevant to WIC/Medicaid Study	Data source
Kotelchuck, Schwartz Anderka and Finison (1984)	Demographics of pregnant non-WIC participants were matched with the demographics of WIC participants	Birthweight Infant mortality Gestational age Use of prenatal care	Decrease in percent of low birthweight (6.9 vs. 8.7%). Nonstatistically significant increase in birthweight (3,281 vs. 3,260 grams). Increased WIC participation associated with larger impacts. Decreased infant mortality. Improvement in use of prenatal care	Birth and Death certificate and WIC data for 8,252 WIC and non-WIC 1978 births in Massachusetts
Metcoff, Costiloe, Crosby, Dutta, Sandstead, Milne, Bodwell and Majors (1985)	Randomly assigned comparison group	Birthweight Maternal nutritional status	Increase in birthweight (3,254 vs. 3,173 grams) not significant when woman's midpregnancy weight was controlled for	Clinical data for 824 WIC-eligible pregnant women attending Oklahoma prenatal clinics
Schramm (1985, 1986, 1989)	Medicaid-covered births to WIC nonparticipants	Medicaid costs within 30 days birth for 1980 data; within 45 days for 1982 and 1985-86. Birthweight	For 1980 Medicaid births, $.83 reduction in Medicaid reimbursements for each dollar spent on the prenatal WIC program; $.49 and $.79 in 1982 and 1985–1986 respectively	7,628 Medicaid births in Missouri in 1980; 9,086 Medicaid births in 1982; and 17,944 Medicaid births in 1985 and 1986

TABLE 19 (Continued).

Study	Comparison groups	Selected outcomes examined	Summary of reported impacts on the outcomes relevant to WIC/Medicaid Study	Data source
Stockbauer (1986, 1987)	Non-WIC births	Birthweight	In 1980, mixed effects on birthweight (depending on method of comparison), with consistently more favorable outcomes among black WIC participants; 1982 found small but consistently favorable effects. Both studies found that at least 7 months of participation were required to observe improved birthweight	1986 study used 1980 data on 6,372 births to prenatal WIC participants in Missouri and from 5,574 to 6,657 non-WIC births; 1987 study used 1982 data on 9,411 WIC and 9,411 non-WIC births
Caan, Horgan, Margess, King, and Jewell (1987)	WIC participants who received postpartum benefits for less than 2 months	Birthweight of first and second pregnancy Birthlength Likelihood of low birthweight Mother's hemoglobin level Pregnancy weight gain	WIC participants of 5–7 months had higher mean birthweight (131g), longer birth birthlength (.3cm) and lower risk of low birthweight. Mothers had higher mean hemoglobin level, and lower risk of maternal obesity	1987 study using 703 WIC participants from California WIC program. Participants broken into two groups: those who received postpartum care between 0-2 months, and those who received postpartum care between 5-7 months

TABLE 19 (Continued).

Study	Comparison groups	Selected outcomes examined	Summary of reported impacts on the outcomes relevant to WIC/Medicaid Study	Data source
Rush (1987)	Low-income, first time non-WIC registrants at prenatal clinics	Birthweight Gestational age Fetal mortality Infant length and head circumference Health behaviour (smoking and use of alcohol) Maternal dietary intake Weight gain	No effect on birthweight, although increased birthweight is significantly related to better program quality. Decrease in fetal deaths and rate of low birthweight of appreciable but not significant magnitude. Statistically significant increase in infant head circumference. No effect on mean gestational age. Reduction in the rate of preterm delivery although not statistically significant. Increased intake of 4 of the 5 nutrients targeted by WIC	5,205 prenatal WIC participants and 1,358 comparisons from 174 WIC sites and 55 prenatal clinics across the country

TABLE 19 (Continued).

Study	Comparison groups	Selected outcomes examined	Summary of reported impacts on the outcomes relevant to WIC/Medicaid Study	Data source
Devaney, Billheimer, and Schore (1991)	All Medicaid-covered births to WIC nonparticipants in 5 states	Medicaid costs for mothers and newborns within 60 days after birth. Birthweight. Likelihood of low birthweight. Gestational age. Likelihood of preterm birth	For each dollar spent on WIC, reduction in Medicaid costs during first 60 days after birth that range from $1.77 to $3.13 for newborns and mothers, and $2.84 to $3.90 for newborns only. Statistically significant increase in birthweight and gestational age. Decrease in the likelihood of preterm birth and low birthweight	1989 study using 1987 data on 111,958 total Medicaid births in Florida, Minnesota, North Carolina, South Carolina and Texas.
Devaney and Schirm (1993)	All Medicaid-covered births to WIC nonparticipants in 5 states	Infant mortality rate	Prenatal WIC participation is associated with decreases in the probability of an infant death in 4 of 5 states examined. Estimated reductions range from 3.6 deaths per 1000 in Florida to 27.2 deaths per 1000 in South Carolina. This latter estimate is outside the possible range.	1993 study using 1987 data on 111,958 total Medicaid births in Florida, Minnesota, North Carolina, South Carolina and Texas.

Source: Extended from table in Devaney, Billheimer and Schore, The Savings in Medicaid Costs for Newborns and Their Mothers From Prenatal Participation in the WIC Program, United States Department of Agriculture.

improve children's nutritional status. Finally, comparisons of the National School Lunch Program (NSLP) and the School Breakfast Program (SBP) suggest that programs with stricter Federal guidelines have greater nutritional effects.

A. WIC

i) Effects on Infant Health and Medicaid Costs

Table 19 summarizes several studies that have evaluated the effects of WIC on infant health. The studies all suggest that WIC has positive effects, although there are differences in the exact conclusions reached: for example, Edozien *et al.* (1979), Kennedy *et al.* (1982), and Metcoff *et al.* (1985) find increases in mean birthweight, while Rush (1987) finds no change in mean birthweight but does find a decrease in the incidence of low birthweight. Devaney and Schirm (1993) also find that prenatal WIC participation is associated with a reduction in infant mortality rates.

Two sets of studies in Table 19 (Schramm (1985, 1986, 1989) and Devaney *et al.* (1990)) examine the effects of WIC on the Medicaid costs of newborns. The results are of particular interest because they can be used to compare the costs and benefits of the WIC program. Schramm found that in 1980 a dollar spent on WIC reduced Medicaid costs in Missouri by about $.80 in the first 30 to 45 days after birth.

Devaney *et al.* examine Medicaid costs in the first 60 days after birth. They study all Medicaid-covered births in Florida, Minnesota, North Carolina, and South Carolina in 1987, as well as births from January through June 1988 in Texas. Altogether there are 105,000 births.[44] The authors compare women who were enrolled in WIC to those who were not. Limiting the study to Medicaid eligibles is likely to eliminate some but not all of the observed and unobserved differences between WIC participants and nonparticipants: for example even among Medicaid eligibles, African-Americans and Native Americans were more likely to participate in WIC than whites. WIC participants were defined as those who participated at any point in the nine months prior to the birth.

---

[44] The study differed from Schramm's both in terms of scale, and because the authors control for the adequacy of prenatal care in all of their models. They argue that by controlling for the adequacy of prenatal care, they are eliminating one possible source of unobserved differences between WIC participants and non-participants. However, since WIC participation and prenatal care may be simultaneously chosen, it is not clear that prenatal care can be legitimately included in the model.

TABLE 20
Estimated Benefit-Cost Ratios

	Estimated savings in Medicaid costs[2]	Estimated prenatal WIC costs per participant	Estimated Benefit cost ratios[1]
Florida			
Newborns and Mothers	$347	$196	1.77
Minnesota			
Newborns and Mothers	$277	$151	1.83
North Carolina			
Newborns	$744	$191	3.90
Newborns and Mothers	$598	$191	3.13
South Carolina[3]			
Newborns and Mothers	$565	$232	2.44
Texas			
Newborns	$573	$202	2.84
Newborns and Mothers	$493	$202	2.44

Notes:
1 Medicaid costs are from birth to 60 days after birth.
2 All estimates are statistically significant at the .01 level (two-tail test), except in Minnesota, where the estimate is statistically significant at the .07 level (two-tail test) and at the .03 level (one-tail test).
3 Medicaid costs refer to hospital costs only.

Source: WIC/Medicaid database for Florida, Minnesota, North Carolina, South Carolina, and Texas.

The results show that WIC participants had an average of 1 to 2 more prenatal visits than non-participants. Their children also had small increases in birthweights. Interestingly, the largest gains in birthweight accrued to babies of less than 37 weeks gestation who are most at risk of complications of low birthweight: these babies gained up to half a pound. WIC participation was also associated with a reduction in prematurity and longer gestational ages.

These improvements had dramatic implications for Medicaid costs. The average costs for newborns and their mothers in the 60 days after birth ranged from $2433 to $3822 depending on the state. The reductions in Medicaid costs associated with WIC participation ranged from $277 to $598. As Table 20 shows, these reductions more than offset the costs of providing WIC to these women.

Of the studies reviewed in Table 19, only Metcoff *et al.* (1985) and Caan *et al.* (1987) used random assignment to generate a comparison group. As

discussed in Chapter 1, studies that do not use random assignment suffer
from the fact that participants may differ from non-participants in unobserved ways. If WIC participants are worse off than non-participants because places are scarce and only the neediest are admitted into the program,
then the studies discussed above may under-estimate the effects of the program. Conversely, if WIC participants are more highly motivated or better
informed than non-participants, then these studies may over-estimate the
program's effects.

Without knowing more about the selection mechanism underlying participation in the program it is difficult to assess the probable direction of
this bias. However, the factors governing selection into the WIC program
are likely to differ considerably over time and across sites. These factors
include the probability of a doctor referral, the extent to which WIC places
are rationed, the amount of advertising, the location of WIC providers, and
so on. Hence, the fact that the estimated effects are remarkably consistent
across samples drawn from different states and at different times suggests
that the positive results are not entirely driven by the selection of women
who are likely to have good outcomes into the program.

A second problem that is pervasive in the WIC literature is that it is difficult to determine the optimal length of prenatal WIC participation. This is
an important question because if it were found, for example, that infants of
women who received WIC only in their third trimester did not benefit from
the program, then it might be optimal to target resources currently expended
on these women to women in their first trimester of pregnancy. The difficulty arises because the length of WIC participation is highly correlated
with the length of gestation. Women with pre-term babies are likely to have
fewer weeks of WIC participation than those with full-term babies. Alternatively, women who do not enter the program until their 9th month are no
longer at risk of bearing a pre-term infant and so may appear to have healthier
infants.

ii) WIC and Nutrition

Fraker (1990) uses the 1985 Continuing Survey of Food Intakes by Individuals to assess the effects of WIC supplementation on the nutritional status of children. Only households with women 19 to 50 years of age were
included in the survey. The women were asked to record the food intakes of
any children 1 to 5 in the day prior to the survey. Fraker excludes children
who were not WIC-eligible. Additional exclusions due to missing data result in a sample of 818 children.

TABLE 21
Statistics on Dietary Intake of WIC Eligible Children
Who are Non-participants in WIC or Food Stamps

	Mean	*SD*
Food Energy NAR[1] (%)	94.6	35.0
Protein NAR (%)	208.1	80.3
% Energy from Protein	15.6	3.8
% Energy from Fat	33.8	8.2
% Energy from Carb.	50.6	9.5
Cholesterol (mg)	225.8	178.8
VITAMINS		
Vitamin A NAR (%)	172.9	113.3
Thiamin NAR (%)	137.1	55.0
Riboflavin NAR (%)	184.0	73.3
Vitamin B6 NAR (%)	112.3	59.8
Vitamin B12 NAR (%)	172.7	96.9
Vitamin C NAR (%)	169.6	152.5
Vitamin E NAR (%)	86.9	53.5
Niacin NAR (%)	130.5	59.6
Folacin NAR (%)	137.7	80.4
MINERALS		
Calcium NAR (%)	101.2	48.0
Phosphorous NAR (%)	122.6	46.9
Magnesium NAR (%)	111.2	42.5
TRACE ELEMENTS		
Iron NAR (%)	67.5	36.9
Zinc NAR (%)	70.4	30.1
Number of Observations	355	

Notes:
[1] NAR is the nutrient adequacy ratio = intake/RDA. All NARs have been converted to percentages. All figures are calculated using sample weights.

This table is from Fraker, T., Analyses of the 1985 Continuing Survey of Food Intakes by Individuals, Volume II, Mathematica Policy Research Inc.

He uses a two-step 'selection correction' procedure in order to control for selection into the program. He also controls for enrollment in the Food Stamp Program and for possible interactions between the two programs. As discussed in Chapter 1, it is important for statistical reasons to have variables that explain participation but not intakes and vice-versa. Fraker includes variables describing family structure and housing in the participation equation but not in the second stage nutrient intake equations. Variables that are excluded from the first stage include the mother's height and race. Given that there is no reason to suppose that these variables actually belong in one equation rather than the other, the results must be interpreted with caution.

Table 21 shows the mean nutrient intakes for WIC eligible children who did not participate in either WIC or the Food Stamp Program. The table shows that for most vitamins and minerals even non-participants had intakes that exceeded the US recommended daily allowance (RDA). However an average non-participant lacked food energy (total calories), Vitamin E, iron, and zinc. WIC participants suffered deficits only in iron and zinc intake, and their iron intakes were 13% closer to the US RDA.

OLS regressions suggest that these differences in food energy, vitamin E, and iron intakes between WIC participants and non-participants are statistically significant even after observable characteristics are controlled for. The two-step estimation procedure described above generally produced larger point estimates, but even larger standard errors.

Another way to control for selection effects is to follow the same child over time. The Centers for Disease Control (1978) report the results of a study that followed child WIC participants in 6 states over a two year interval. They found that after 3 WIC visits the percent of children who were anemic fell from 23% to 10% among children 6 to 23 months of age, and from 24% to 12% among children 24 to 59 months old. In addition, 21% of 6- to 23-month-old children entering the program were below the tenth percentile of length-for-age – after three WIC visits, only 15% of these children were below this cutoff.[45]

iii)WIC Effects on Later Cognitive Development

Hicks et al. (1982) report suggestive results from a small-scale study of the effects of WIC participation on later cognitive development. They note that previous studies have established a link between severe malnutrition, protein deficiencies, or anemia, and cognitive deficits. The question is to what extent the less severe malnutrition or anemia that might be present in a US population of poor children presents a threat to child development?

The study focuses on 21 pairs of siblings from rural Louisiana. Because of the design of the WIC program in that state, the younger child in each pair was eligible for supplementation beginning in the third trimester of pregnancy, while the older child became eligible for WIC only after the first

---

[45] Among very young children it is easier to measure length-for-age than height-for-age. However, the interpretation is similar.

year. The results show that the 'early supplementation' group had significantly higher scores on tests of verbal ability and IQ, and on a 'Draw-A-
Person' test.

It is possible that these results are biased by the fact that it was always
the younger child who received the early supplementation. However, when
the authors use measures that were taken when the two children were the
same age, such as their grade point averages in grade one and their heights-
for-age, they still find that early supplementation has a significant effect.
They note that in general there is a slight negative association between par-
ity and IQ, so the finding that the younger children had higher IQs is unlikely to be solely an artifact of birth order.

B. School Nutrition Programs.

Given the size, age, and national character of the school lunch and breakfast
programs there has been surprisingly little evaluation. In 1979 a bi-partisan
Senate committee requested the Secretary of Agriculture to commission a
study. This resulted in the National Evaluation of School Nutrition Programs (NESNP), which surveyed students, parents, and school food service
administrators.

i) Effects on Nutrition

Hanes *et al.* (1984) use the NESNP to compare the nutritional content of the
breakfasts and lunches of participants and non-participants. They also examine nutrient intakes over a 24 hour period in order to assess the extent to
which families compensate for school meals by reducing the child's home
food consumption. They find that school lunches contain more of almost all
the nutrients that were examined than non-participant lunches. In part, this
is due to a higher calorie content, but school lunches are also more nutritious. In addition, school lunch participants have higher 24 hour nutrient
intakes, which indicates that families do not entirely offset the effects of
food supplementation.

School breakfasts contain more calcium, phosphorus, protein, and mag-
nesium than other breakfasts. But they have less vitamin A, B, Niacin, thia-
min and iron. Children who have a school breakfast have higher 24 hour
intakes of calcium and phosphorus than those who have another breakfast,
which indicates that the initial gains in other nutrients are offset over the
course of the day. However, the availability of a school breakfast does have
a positive effect on the probability that a child eats breakfast, and children

who eat breakfast have higher 24 hour nutrient intakes of most nutrients than children who do not.

Vermeersch *et al.* (1984) examine the effects of the NSLP and the SBP on child anthropometry. They find that among younger children (males under 11.5 and females under 10 years) fewer school lunch participants fall below the 25th percentile of weight-for-height. They did not find any significant effect of the SBP.

The differences in the effects of the NSLP and the SBP on nutrient intakes probably reflect differences in Federal standards. Lunches must conform to 'meal patterns' that specify the types, amounts, and methods of preparation of food. The nutritional content of lunches averaged over some period of time must supply one-third of the US RDA for children of various ages. By and large, the lunches served appear to meet these standards.

The standards for breakfasts are much looser, perhaps because the government wishes to encourage school districts to participate. The two nutrients that are consumed in greater quantities over a 24 hour period by school breakfast participants are both found in milk, which is a compulsory component of the breakfast meal pattern (Radkowski and Gale, 1984b). Hence, it seems that the effectiveness of the school nutrition programs is directly related to the strictness of the federal guidelines governing them.

ii) Effects on Cognitive Achievement

Meyers *et al.* (1988) examined 1,092 third to sixth grade children in Lawrence, Massachusetts, before and after the SBP was introduced in their school in 1987. They found that the Breakfast Program participants showed greater improvements in test scores, relative to their initial scores, than non-participant children. Breakfast Program participation also reduced tardiness.

iii) Participation and Family Food Expenditures

In principle, families can offset the effects of the school nutrition programs by feeding their children less at home. To the extent that families do offset, a dollar of food served at school will purchase less than an additional dollar of food for the child. The evidence on this question is mixed. Evaluations of the SBP (West and Price, 1976; Wellisch *et al.*, 1983a,b; Maurer, 1984; Devaney and Fraker, 1987; Long, 1987) find that there is no effect of participation in SBP on family food expenditures. Studies of the NSLP suggest that the offset ranges from zero (Wellisch *et al.*, 1983a,b; Maurer, 1984) to about half (West and Price, 1976; Devaney and Fraker, 1987; Long, 1987).

All but 2 of these studies (West and Price, 1976; and Devaney and Fraker, 1987) are based on the NESNP data, so the range of estimates reflects methodological differences. The studies differ in terms of whether NSLP and SBP expenditures are counted in total household expenditures and in their treatment of control variables. In particular, studies that account for the age and sex of household members by scaling household expenditures using equivalence scales tend to get higher offsets than those that incorporate demographic information in other ways.

As we saw in Chapter 3, the average SBP participants tends to be much poorer than the average NSLP participant. Hence, it would not be surprising if the extent of the offset were greater for the richer group. To see this, suppose that families of SBP participants are purchasing less food than they would like. Then the addition of a free school breakfast is unlikely to have any effect on other food expenditures. On the other hand, some better-off NSLP families may already be purchasing as much food as they need, so that the addition of a reduced price school lunch causes them to shift expenditures from food to other goods. It is possible that the .5 estimates represent an average over poor NLSB households that do not offset and somewhat better-off NLSB households that do. One way to get this issue would be to estimate offsets by income level.

The studies also differ in whether or not they attempt to take selection into the programs into account. Participation is related to the school meal price, household size, and whether there is an adult who eats meals at home (Maurer, 1984b). However, since these variables may be related to child nutrition (meal price for example, depends on the household's income) it is not clear that they can be included in the particpation equation and excluded from the nutrient intake equations.

C. Other Child Nutrition Programs

Little research has been done on the effects of other child nutrition programs, perhaps because they are so much smaller than the school nutrition programs. The Summer Food Program (SFP), which is administered through schools, reaches about 1.6 million children per day while the Child Care Food Program (CCFP) reaches 1.2 million (Parker, 1989). USDA evaluations have shown that meals provided by the SFP meet one-third of the US RDAs and that meals served by child care centers participating in the CCFP are significantly more nutritious than those served in centers that do not participate (USDA 1988, 1983).

D. Summary

Some of the individual studies reviewed are flawed by a failure to adequately account for selection into the programs. But together they present compelling evidence that food supplementation programs like WIC, NSLP, and SBP can improve pregnancy outcomes and child nutrition. These studies provide support for the notion that programs targeted directly to children can attain specific goals.

Studies of the SBP suggest that it is very efficient in the sense that every dollar spent represents a dollar's worth of food in the stomach of a poor child. Studies of the NSLP suggest that this program is less efficient, probably because it serves a much larger and less narrowly targeted population. One caveat is that most studies of the school nutrition program are based on data from the early 80s. It is not clear what effect reductions in expenditures per child over the decade have had on the program.

8. HEAD START

Head Start has been billed as 'a proven success that gives disadvantaged children a chance to get ahead' (Clinton and Gore, 1992). Yet despite remarkable bi-partisan support, the program is not without detractors who claim that its benefits have been vastly overstated (cf. Borden and O'Beirne, 1989). Given incontrovertible evidence of short-run gains to IQ, the argument centers on whether Head Start has any lasting effects.

The debate is hampered by the fact that despite the broad goals of the Head Start program, most evaluations have focused only on effects on test scores. This chapter reviews the available evidence about the short and long-term effects of Head Start and assesses what we know about the effects of Head Start on children's cognition, health, and schooling attainment.

A. Short-term Effects of Head Start

As discussed above, most evaluations of the Head Start program have focused on measures of IQ and other measures of cognitive achievement. A 'meta-analysis'[46] of 72 studies conducted by the US Department of

---

[46] Meta-analysis is a technique for summarizing data from many individual studies. See Hunter and Schmidt (1990).

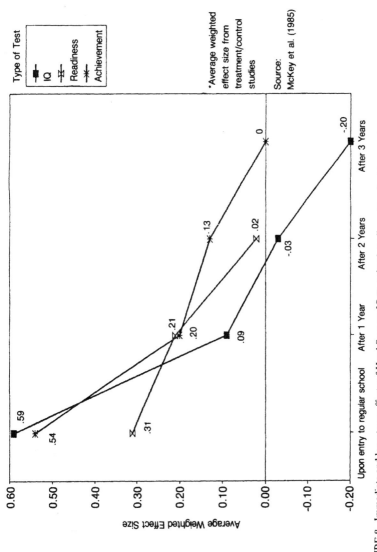

FIGURE 8 Immediate and long-term effects of Head Start on IQ ■, school readiness x and achievement measures *

Source: McKey *et al.* (1985).

Health and Human Services (McKey *et al.*, 1985)[47] is summarized in
Figure 8. The figure shows the weighted average effect of participation in
Head Start from the subset of studies that used an experimental treatment
and control design.[48] The scale was chosen so that gains of .25 or greater
can be thought of as educationally meaningful in the sense that they are
accompanied by noticeable improvement in classroom performance. Hence
the figure shows large gains upon entry to regular school that dissipate rapidly. McKey *et al.* (1985) note that the sources of these gains are not well
understood. Studies that have examined the effects of different types of cur-
ricula, class size, length of the school day, racial and ethnic composition of
the class, and type of program administration have produced weak or con-
flicting results.

Another short-term gain provided by Head Start is improved access to
health services. Thirty-four studies reviewed by McKey *et al.* provide qualitative evidence that children in Head Start are more likely than non-participants to receive routine checkups, dental care, and screenings for speech,
language, developmental delays, vision, and hearing.

Using data from the National Longitudinal Survey's Child-Mother file
(NLSCM), Currie and Thomas (1993b) provide quantitative analyses of the
effects of Head Start participation on the probability of having been immunized against measles as of 1990 and on height-for-age. Head Start aims to
'provide a comprehensive health services program which includes a broad
range of medical services. . .'including' an assessment of immunization
status'. The Head Start program performance standards also state that 'every
child in a part-day program will receive a quantity of food in meals. . . and
snacks which provides at least 1/3 of daily nutritional needs. . .' (Head Start
Bureau, 1992). Both nutritious food and better medical care are expected to
improve child growth. Hence, there is some reason to expect a positive ef-

---

[47] There have been several other surveys of the Head Start literature. See Westinghouse Learning Corporation and Ohio University (1969), Bronfenbrenner (1975), Datta (1979), Horowitz
and Paden (1973), and White (1985-86). Vinovskis (1993) shows that the debate about the
efficacy of compensatory education in the US dates back at least to the 1840s when 40% of all
three-year-olds in Massachusetts were attending infant schools.

[48] Studies that make use of the kind of quasi-experimental design discussed in Chapter 2 are
excluded. In many cases, the comparison children in these studies were drawn from waiting
lists for the Head Start program. There is anecdotal evidence that local staff select the most
disadvantaged children to participate. If this is true, then studies that rely on this design could
understate the effect of Head Start (Haskins, 1989). Lee, Brooks-Gunn and Schnur (1988)
reanalyzed data on Head Start children and two groups of 'controls' and found that the Head
Start group had less educated mothers, which suggests that they may also differ in other respects.

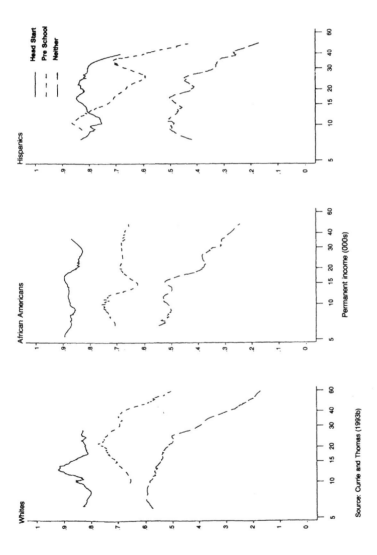

FIGURE 9 Non parametric estimates Pr (Measles Shot)
US Permanent Income by race. Short line = Head Start, Short dash = preschool, Long dash = neither

fect of participation in Head Start on child height as well as on immunization rates.

The NLSCM is a large national sample with information about many
children who attended regular Head Start programs. About 8% of white
children, 16% of Hispanic children and 27% of African-American children
were enrolled. It is also possible to identify children who attended other
types of preschool programs and to compare their outcomes with those of
the Head Start children. These children may be a more relevant comparison
group than children who attend no preschool since they are also cared for in
group settings away from home.

Figure 9 shows non-parametric estimates of the relationship between Head
Start and preschool status, permanent income[49], and immunization status in
1990. The figure shows that for white and African-American children, the
probability of having been immunized against measles is significantly higher
at all levels of permanent income for children who were in Head Start relative to those who went to other preschools.[50] The latter are, in turn, more
likely to have been immunized than those who did not attend any preschool.
Among Hispanics, the large differences are between those who went to Head
Start or another preschool and those who did not.[51] Thus, for all three ethnic
groups, those who did not attend any preschool are the least likely to have
been immunized.

Figure 10 shows that white children who attended preschools are taller
than other children.[52] There is little difference between those who attended
Head Start and those who did not attend any preschool. Among African-
Americans, children who attended Head Start are very close, in terms of

---

[49] Currie and Thomas (1993b) define permanent income as the logarithm of average annual
household income between 1978 and 1990 (in real 1990 dollars). Use of this measure should
attenuate the influence of measurement error and breaks the link between household income
at a point in time and eligibility for the Head Start program. Household permanent income is
about $29,000 for the average white child, $23,000 for Hispanics and $18,000 for African-
Americans in this sample.

[50] Figures 9 and 10 show locally-weighted smoothed scatterplots (LOWESS) (Cleveland, 1979)
which are a nearest neighbor-type estimator. Essentially, each observation is replaced by its
predicted value based on a weighted regression using the observations in a band around it.
Hence the shape of the estimated function is determined locally throughout the distribution of
income (See, also, Hardle, 1990).

[51] All these differences are statistically significant at the 95% level of confidence.

[52] The difference in means is statistically significant at the 95% level of confidence.

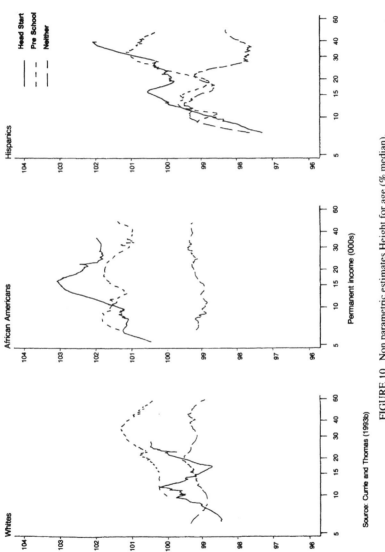

FIGURE 10 Non parametric estimates Height for age (% median).
US Permanent Income by race. Short line = Head Start, Short dash = preschool, Long dash = neither

Source: Currie and Thomas (1993b)

height, to those who attended preschools and both these groups of children are taller than the other children. The differences among Hispanics are less clear although at the top of the income distribution we see that Hispanic children who attended either Head Start or preschool tend to be taller than other Hispanic children.

These correlations between health and Head Start or preschool enrollment status may reflect selection into the program: taller and healthier children may be more likely to be enrolled in programs outside the home. A great advantage of the NLSCM is that differences between family backgrounds of Head Start children and non-Head Start children can be controlled for by comparing the outcomes of children who were enrolled to those of siblings who were not. As discussed in Chapter 1, this procedure controls for the many relatively constant aspects of family background.

Currie and Thomas (1993b) show that in models with fixed effects, participation in Head Start is associated with increases in the probabilities that white and African-American children receive measles shots of 10% and 12%, respectively. For whites, the effects of Head Start and other preschool participation are equal, while for African-Americans Head Start attendance has a larger effect. Head Start is not estimated to have a statistically significant effect on the probability that a Hispanic child is immunized, but the hypothesis that Head Start and other preschool attendance have the same effect cannot be rejected.

B. Longer-term Effects of Head Start

i) Evidence from Model Preschool Programs

The most widely cited evidence in support of the long-term benefits of Head Start actually comes from studies of model preschool programs such as the Perry Preschool Project or the Tennessee Early Training Project. These programs were funded at higher levels, involved more intensive interventions, and had better-trained staff than the typical Head Start program. Furthermore, many of these studies involved very small samples: for example, the Perry Preschool Project followed 58 treatments and 65 controls (Berrueta-Clement et al., 1984).

Still, the results of the Perry Preschool Project are striking: children who went through the program were one third more likely to graduate from highschool, 50% more likely to be employed or in post-secondary education after highschool, half as likely to have a teen pregnancy, and 40% less likely to have been arrested. The question is, whether these kinds of gains can be attributed to the Head Start program?

ii) Effects on Vocabulary

Although most previous studies find no long-term evidence of gains to cognitive achievement, Currie and Thomas (1993b) find that there are gains to the percentile Peabody Picture Vocabulary (PPVT) scores of white and Hispanic children among children over 8 years old who had attended Head Start. Estimates from models of PPVT that include sibling fixed effects are shown in Table 22.[53] The difference between these results and those of previous studies may be due to the fact that previous studies have not disaggregated by race and ethnicity. There are no significant gains to percentile PIAT Mathematics or PIAT Reading Comprehension scores among children in this age group.

iii) Effects on Schooling Attainment

McKey *et al.* (1985) note that very few studies have examined the impact of Head Start on retention in grade, or on the probability of being placed in remedial education. These include: McDonald and Monroe (undated), Goodstein, Cawley, and Burrows (1975), Consortium (1983), Copple, Cline, and Smith (1987), Bee (1981) and Hebbeler (1987). These studies find generally positive effects of participation in Head Start. For example, Copple, Cline, and Smith (1987) followed children in 33 Philadelphia schools up to grade 6. They found that children who had participated in Head Start were less likely to have repeated a grade or to have been placed in remedial education. They also had better attendance and were more likely to be present when standardized tests were administered.[54]

Table 23 shows estimates of the probability of repeating a grade from models with sibling fixed effects taken from Currie and Thomas (1993b). The estimates indicate that participation in Head Start reduces the probability that white and Hispanic children repeat grades, but appears to have no

---

[53] The PIATs were administered to all children of five and over, and were administered to many children in more than on wave of the survey. In cases where there are repeated measures Currie and Thomas use the mean score in order to attenuate the influence of random measurement error. The PPVT was administered to all children of three and over, but due to budget constraints, was typically only administered once per child.

[54] The results of Copple, Cline and Smith may be severely biased by attrition from the sample, since 70% of the students were lost by the time they reached the sixth grade.

TABLE 22
Head Start and Other Preschool Effects on Test Scores
from Models that Include Mother Fixed Effects
for Children >=8 Years Old

	White			African-American			Hispanic		
	PIAT MATH	PIAT READING	PPVT	PIAT MATH	PIAT READING	PPVT	PIAT MATH	PIAT READING	PPVT
Head Start	2.83 (.74)	2.11 (.49)	9.30 (2.10)	-1.45 (.52)	-.38 (0.12)	-2.16 (.87)	.99 (.22)	7.10 (1.35)	9.92 (2.58)
Other Preschool	5.77 (2.03)	1.00 (.33)	.22 (.07)	5.44 (1.64)	2.92 (.79)	2.82 (.97)	-.91 (.18)	-.53 (.09)	3.14 (.75)
# Observations	912	754	967	736	662	718	385	321	391
R-squared	.74	.75	.81	.71	.73	.77	.67	.66	.82
Mean Dep. Var.	50.39	54.66	41.45	36.98	43.64	16.43	39.19	45.43	20.18

Notes:
T-statistics in parentheses. These regressions also included the log of income when each child was age 3, a dummy variable equal to 1 if the child was male, the child's age in months in 1990, and a dummy variable equal to one if the child was the first born.

Source: Currie and Thomas (1993b).

effect on African-American children. Attendance at a non-Head Start pre-school has no effect on the probability of grade repetition.

C. Discussion

i) Biases in Estimates Based on Sibling Differences

As discussed in Chapter 1, in the presence of measurement error, differencing may result in 'throwing the baby out with the bath water', since the true 'signal' may be discarded while the 'noise' remains. A second problem is that estimates with household fixed effects are based on households in which one child attended Head Start and the other did not. If there are any spillover effects of Head Start from one sibling to the other, then the difference between the two siblings will underestimate the effect of the program. Spillover effects might be important either because a child teaches his or her sibling something learned in Head Start, or because the parent learns something or gains access to a service that is beneficial to both children. Conversely, a negative shock to a family that made one child eligible for Head Start could have an adverse impact on the other child, even if that child was not eligible for Head Start because of age. These arguments both suggest that estimates based on sibling comparisons may be lower bounds on the true program effects.

Alternatively, factors specific to a given child may be important. Suppose, for example, that a parent systematically favored the sibling that was in Head Start. In this case, the estimated Head Start effect from [4] would be an over-estimate of the true program effect.

ii) Differences by Race and Ethnicity

Why do the effects of Head Start appear to vary so greatly with race? The estimates discussed above suggest that once selection into the program is taken into account, Head Start has a smaller effect on the test scores and schooling attainment of African-Americans than on the test scores and academic achievement of white and Hispanic children. This finding is all the more striking because in terms of health, African-American children appear to gain as much from Head Start as other children. African-Americans are as likely as white children to be vaccinated if they are in Head Start, and they are more likely to experience gains in height-for-age.

Why do race and ethnicity matter? One hypothesis is that there is heterogeneity in the Head Start programs that serve children of different races. It

TABLE 23
Head Start Effects on Grade Repetition,
from Models that Include Mother Fixed Effects,
for Children >= 10 Years Old

	White	African American	Hispanic
Head Start	-.51	-.03	-.46
	(2.27)	(.31)	(2.96)
Other Preschool	-.08	-.17	-.005
	(.67)	(1.34)	(.02)
Log income	.08	-.14	-.38
at Age 3	(.75)	(1.10)	(2.04)
Male	-.06	-.13	-.01
	(.97)	(1.93)	(.09)
Age in months	.004	-.001	.01
1990	(1.45)	(.35)	(1.91)
First born	-.13	.05	-.16
	(1.35)	(.57)	(1.20)
# Observations	269	311	141
R-squared	.63	.59	.65
Mean Dep. Var.	.36	.47	.32

Notes:
T-statistics in parentheses.

Source: Currie and Thomas (1993b).

is possible that programs that serve African-Americans place more emphasis on health and less emphasis on academic achievement than programs
serving white and Hispanic children. Given limited budgets, such a focus
might be justified if African-American children typically came into the program in worse health.

An alternative hypothesis is that the benefits of compensatory education
depend both on the program itself and on the child's home background including, for example, the level of resources at home, as well as the type and
quality of school attended after Head Start. To the extent that African-American children come disproportionately from more disadvantaged homes, located in poorer communities, and attend troubled schools, one might expect
Head Start to have smaller effects. Thus, race may be a proxy for a disadvantaged background.

On the other hand, since the average Hispanic child in this sample also comes from a disadvantaged background relative to a white child, one must explain the beneficial effects of Head Start on the test scores and academic achievement of these children. It is possible that children with English-language difficulties benefit disproportionately from the early opportunity to learn in an English-language setting.

In order to separate out the effects of race and ethnicity and the effects of a disadvantaged family background, Currie and Thomas (1993b) pool children from the three racial and ethnic groups and limit the analysis to children in families with permanent incomes greater than $10,000 and less than $18,000. The $10,000 cutoff marks the 6th percentile of the white income distribution, the 26th percentile of the African-American income distribution, and the 12th percentile of the Hispanic distribution in their sample. The $18,000 cutoff marks the 28th, 64th, and 45th percentiles of the white, African-American, and Hispanic distributions, respectively. They find that even in this subsample, Head Start participation lowers the probability of retention in grade more for whites than for African-Americans.

D. Summary

Participation in Head Start is associated with better performance on standardized tests among whites and Hispanics. These effects persist for children 8 years and older. White and Hispanic children are less likely to have repeated a grade if they attended Head Start and white children are more likely to receive measles shots.

In contrast, African-Americans who attended Head Start do not appear to perform better on tests or in school. They do, however, seem to do better in terms of health: they are more likely to receive measles shots and are significantly taller than their siblings who did not attend a preschool.

There are then, dramatic racial and ethnic differences in the effects of Head Start. These differences cannot be entirely explained by observable differences in household resources such as permanent income. Further investigation of the reasons for these differences is likely to provide insights that will make Head Start a more effective program.

CHART 1
HUD's Definition of Deficient Housing

Severely Deficient Housing
- lacks hot or cold water or a flush toilet, or both a bathtub *and* a shower.
- heating equipment has broken down at least 3 times for 6 hours or more, resulting in the unit being uncomfortably cold for 24 hours or more.
- no electricity, or exposed wiring *and* a room with no working wall outlet *and* 3 blown fuses or tripped circuit-breakers during the previous 90 days.
- public areas such as hallways and stairs have no working light fixtures *and* loose or missing steps *and* loose or missing railings *and* no elevators.
- at least 5 basic maintenance problems such as water leaks, holes in floors or ceilings, peeling paint or broken plaster, or evidence of rats.

Moderately Deficient Housing
- on at least 3 occasions in the past 3 months, all flush toilets were broken for at least 6 hours.
- unvented gas, oil, or kerosene heaters are its primary heating equipment.
- lacks a sink, refrigerator, or either burners or an oven.
- 3 of the 4 hallway or staircase problems listed above.
- 3 of the basic maintenance problems listed above.

Source: Lazere (1991).

9. HOUSING ASSISTANCE

Since the Housing Act of 1949, Congress has periodically reaffirmed the national goal of providing a 'decent home and suitable living environment for every American family'. The most recent expression of this concern was embodied in the National Affordable Housing Act of 1990. This chapter explores the extent to which this goal has been met, discusses the role of neighborhoods and schools in children's lives, and concludes with an assessment of the extent to which federal housing policies are successful in meeting the needs of families with children.

A. Adequate Housing for All?

i) *Severely and Moderately Deficient Housing*
While the quality of the housing stock has shown steady improvement over time, there are still many housing units that the Department of Housing and Development (HUD) classifies as either severely or moderately deficient.

HUD's definitions of deficient housing are given in Chart 1. In 1989, 18% of poor households, or 2.2 million poor households, lived in housing with severe or moderate physical problems. In contrast, 7% of non-poor households lived in such housing.

Obviously deficient housing can pose a hazard to children's health. Poor sanitation and heating can lead to an increase in common childhood illnesses, which if untreated, can result in permanent disabilities. For example, recurrent ear infections can lead to hearing losses. Diseases such as lead poisoning are also directly related to housing conditions. Finally, we saw in Chapter 2 that poor children were at three times the risk of accidental death of non-poor children. Some of this increased risk may be due to hazards in their homes.

ii) *Unaffordable Housing*

Unaffordable housing is a greater problem than deficient housing in the sense that it affects a greater number of families. Standards set by federal law define affordable housing as housing that consumes no more than 30% of a household's 'adjusted' income.[55] Recall that the federal poverty line assumes that households spend approximately a third of their income on food. Hence, the federal guidelines envisage that a family at the poverty line would spend 30% of its income on food, 30% on housing, and 40% on everything else. In reality, three quarters of poor households in the US paid over 30% of their income for housing in 1989, and more than half spent over 50% (Lazere *et al.*, 1991). There is a limited amount of evidence that families in these circumstances are forced to cut back on necessities. Meyer *et al.* (1993) report that among low income children attending a Boston clinic, those living in public housing or receiving rent subsidies are significantly less likely to suffer from iron anemia.

Figure 11 shows that one cause of the low-income housing crunch is a decline in the number of low-rent units. Many of these losses are due to the rehabilitation or conversion of units, which highlights the tension between the goals of improving the housing stock and preserving low-rent units. While the number of low-rent units has fallen, the poor have gotten poorer as inequality in the United States has risen and the level of cash welfare

---

[55] Adjustments include deductions for dependent children, handicapped or elderly family members, and for excessive health or child care costs.

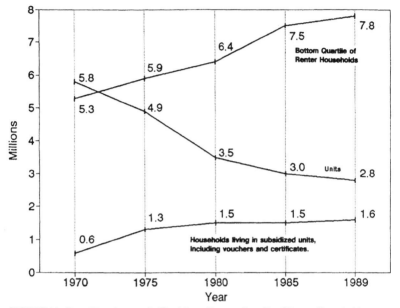

FIGURE 11   Rental housing trends. Top Line = Bottom Quartile of Renter Households,
Middle Line = Low Rent Units, Bottom Line = Households Living in subsidized units.
Source Dolbeare (1992).

Note: Figure from C. Dolbeare, "The Widening Gap: Housing Needs of Low Income Families", Low Income Housing Information Service, June 1992

benefits has fallen. Table 24 shows that in most states, the maximum AFDC
grant for a family of three is less than HUD's estimate of the 'Fair Market
Rent' (FMR) for a two-bedroom apartment. In contrast, in 1975, the maximum AFDC benefit for a family of three exceeded the FMR for a two-
bedroom apartment in 40 states (Lazere et al., 1991).

The lengthy waiting lists for public housing in most cities are another
indicator of the extent of the housing crisis. In 1988, only 24% of AFDC
households received any form of housing assistance. Approximately one
million households were on waiting lists for public housing, while a further
800,000 were on waiting lists for privately owned, subsidized housing
(Lazere et al., 1991). Sixteen percent of the largest housing authorities (those
administering over 2,500 units) are refusing to take new applications. In
San Francisco for example, the waiting list for public housing was closed in

TABLE 24
AFDC Benefits and Housing Costs

State	Maximum benefit, Family of three	Fair market rent, 2 bedroom Apt.
Alabama	$124	390
Alaska	891	550
Arizona	293	570
Arkansas	204	410
California	694	750
Colorado	356	480
Connecticut	680	680
Delaware	338	590
District of Columbia	428	730
Florida	294	520
Georgia	280	500
Hawaii	632	700
Idaho	317	540
Illinois	367	610
Indiana	288	450
Iowa	426	470
Kansas	409	460
Kentucky	228	410
Lousiana	190	470
Maine	453	590
Maryland	406	610
Massachusetts	539	780
Michigan (Wayne Co.)	525	490
Minnesota	532	530
Mississippi	120	430
Missouri	292	450
Montana	370	480
Nebraska	364	440
Nevada	330	680
New Hampshire	516	660
New Jersey	424	650
New Mexico	310	610
New York (New York City)	577	610
North Carolina	272	420
North Dakota	401	440
Ohio	334	440
Oklahoma	341	440
Oregon	444	510
Pennsylvania	421	510
Rhode Island	554	610
South Carolina	210	400
South Dakota	385	430
Tennessee	195	430
Texas	184	460
Utah	402	410

Table 24 (Continued)

State	Maximum benefit, Family of three	Fair market rent, 2 bedroom Apt.
Vermont	679	640
Virginia	354	570
Washington	531	530
West Virginia	249	450
Wisconsin	517	470
Wyoming	360	600

Source: Lazere et al., (1991).

1988 while the list for privately owned subsidized housing was closed in 1986. As of Dec. 1991, 6000 families remained on these lists. The average wait for a family on a waiting list is 18 months to two years (Lazere et al., 1991). However, in New York City, a qualified family joining the waiting list today, could wait more than 20 years for an apartment.

Families that are unable to find housing they can afford face the threat of homelessness. Although estimates vary widely, most observers agree that there are at least 600,000 homeless and that families are the fastest growing group of homeless people. Some estimates place the number of homeless children as high as 300,000 (Hewlitt, 1991). Homelessness can have a devastating effect on children. One study found that compared to other poor children, homeless children had almost double the rate of school problems and school failure, and that they had high rates of other health problems such as developmental delays and overweight. The diets of homeless children were generally poor, characterized by dependence on food from fastfood restaurants and periods of deprivation (Wood et al., 1990). Still, the homeless families in the study had much higher rates of parental drug and alcohol abuse, and of domestic violence so it is not clear that this study isolates the effects of homelessness per se.

B. The Effects of Neighborhoods

Finding a home involves not only selecting a building, but choosing neighborhoods, friends, and schools. Wilson (1987) argues that the poor live in uniquely disadvantaged neighborhoods that offer children few role models and few opportunities for escape from poverty. Furthermore, he argues that the concentration of poverty in specific neighborhoods has increased since the 1970s.[56] These arguments suggest that a housing policy that enabled poor households to move to non-poor neighborhoods could have dramatic effects on the prospects of poor children. However, the effects of neighborhoods and schools remain controversial.

i) *The Non-Experimental Evidence*

In their survey, Mayer and Jencks (1990) identify 3 ways that living in a poor neighborhood can affect a child. The first is the 'epidemic' or 'collective socialization' model. The idea is that if children grow up in a neighborhood where people commit crime, have children out of wedlock, and drop out of school, then they will be more likely to do these things themselves. However, some social scientists dispute this view, pointing out that even in poor neighborhoods it is possible to find good role models. These 'institutionalists' argue that it is not the neighbors but the resources available in the neighborhood, such as the quality of the schools, that matter. Finally, it is sometimes argued that affluent neighbors can actually be a disadvantage for a poor person. For example, a poor child transferred to a wealthy school may be at great academic disadvantage relative to other children. Some may respond to the increased level of difficulty by dropping out.

They summarize the evidence regarding the effects of neighborhoods as follows: teenagers who live in neighborhoods with high socio-economic status (SES) attain more education than children from similar families who live in low SES neighborhoods. Among African-American teenagers, low SES neighborhoods are associated with higher probabilities of teen sexual activity and pregnancy. Highschool students in predominantly African-American schools are more likely to drop out than those in predominantly white schools, even when the student's own race and SES are controlled for. There is also evidence that African-American males who attended mixed highschools are more likely to be employed than those who did not.

The evidence about the effect of the mean SES of children in a highschool on individual test scores and student aspirations is mixed, but it appears that highschool SES has only small effects. For example, in an analysis of the High School and Beyond data set, in which he controls for unobserved char-

---

[56] Bane and Jargowsky (1988) provide empirical support for this hypothesis.

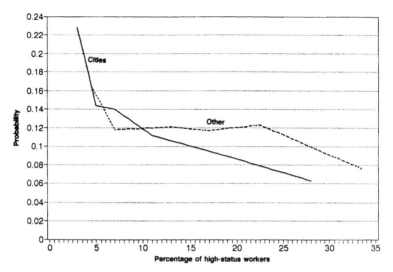

FIGURE 12   Probability of black teenagers dropping out of school as a function of percentage
of high-status workers in the neighborhood, by location of neighborhood.

acteristics of neighborhoods and schools by including fixed effects for each
highschool, Altonji (1988) finds that 'most of the similarity in the educational outcomes of students from the same school appears to be due to the
fact that students with similar backgrounds, aptitude, and achievement have
similar educational outcomes regardless of what school they attend'. Altonji
(1992) also finds that a student's academic track has remarkably little influence on educational attainment or wage rates.

However, it is difficult to draw any causal inferences from non-experimental data because, as Mayer and Jencks point out, 'people who move into
different neighborhoods differ before they arrive, and the people who remain in a given neighborhood differ from those who leave'. Hence, any
relationship we observe between neighborhood characteristics and individual
outcomes could reflect the characteristics of the individual or of his or her
family that drew them to the neighborhood in the first place.

A second problem is that the effects of residence in a low SES
neighborhood may be highly non-linear. That is, it may be only very bad
neighborhoods that have a negative effect on children. Figure 12 shows that
the estimated probability of dropping out of school declines precipitously
as the percentage of workers in the neighborhood with professional or mana-

gerial jobs increases from less than 5% to over 5%, and then falls much more gently as the number of high-status workers increases further (Crane, 1991).

Finally, most studies of 'neighborhood effects' are not very specific about how it is that the neighborhood, or the school, affects the child. This is partly a matter of inadequate data. Whatever one's hypotheses about causality, it is unlikely that the neighborhood that matters to a child is defined in terms of zip codes or census tracts.

One hypothesis that is quite specific about the effect of neighborhoods, holds that African-American teenagers have high unemployment rates because they live in areas with few jobs. Ellwood (1986) investigates this 'spatial mismatch' hypothesis using data from tthe Chicago Area Transportation Study. These data cover 20,000 workers in 116 zones. His findings are striking. First, labor market outcomes for young African-Americans in the West Side ghetto were remarkably similar to those of youths on the South Side, despite dramatic differences in the accessibility of jobs. Second, African-American and white teens who lived in the same neighborhood had unemployment rates that differed just as dramatically as those of African-American and white teenagers who lived across town from each other. The inclusion of neighborhood fixed effects had no impact on the racial differential in employment probabilities.

ii) *The Gautreaux Program*

The Gautreaux program provides an interesting 'natural experiment' that sheds light on these issues. It grew out of a lawsuit filed in 1966 against the Chicago Housing Authority and HUD on behalf of public housing residents. The suit charged that the Chicago low-rent public housing program had been administered in a racially discriminatory manner. A consent decree established by the Supreme Court in 1976, created a unique demonstration program whose aim was to reduce segregation in Chicago's public housing.

Under the program, residents in public housing projects can apply for Section 8 housing certificates and move to private apartments. Some apartments are in predominantly white suburbs, while others are in the inner city. The program assigns apartments in an approximately random manner since although applicants are supposed to have some say in where they will live, the apartments they are offered depend on what the agency has available. Few applicants turn down an offered apartment, because if they do, they are unlikely to be offered another.

Applicants are not entirely typical of public housing residents since they are screened to make sure that they have paid their rent regularly, and that they have adequate housekeeping abilities. The program does not serve families with more than 4 children because few large housing units are available in the suburbs. In addition, the act of applying for an apartment in an unknown location may indicate that a person is strongly motivated to improve his or her circumstances.

Rosenbaum (1982) found that compared to children of participants who moved within the inner city, those who moved to the suburbs attended schools that were superior in terms of smaller class sizes, and satisfaction with teachers and courses. On average, these children had better attitudes towards school, and suffered no permanent decline in grades or attendance. However, some children had trouble meeting higher academic standards in the suburbs and were placed in lower grades, lower tracks, or in remedial education.

The children in the original survey were re-interviewed 7 years later (Rosenbaum (1992)). Unfortunately, only 59% of the original sample children, or 107 children, could be located. Still, the results are suggestive. Children who had moved to the suburbs were 15% less likely to have dropped out of school, 16% more likely to be in a college track program, and 34% more likely to be employed than those who had moved within the inner city. All of these differences were statistically significant at the 90% level of confidence.

Rosenbaum (1992) also reports the results of a survey of mothers who had participated in the program. Sixty-seven percent of those surveyed responded, resulting in a sample of 108 city movers and 224 suburban movers. Although there were no differences between the two groups in history of welfare recipiency, education, or previous work experience, the group that moved to the suburbs was 25% more likely to have a job.

These figures suggest that in at least some cases, moving low-income families to areas with better labor markets and good schools can have positive effects on the life chances of children. But as noted above, the estimates are based on a small sample that has been subjected to some screening. And it is not clear that a program that proved successful for women and children would benefit jobless youths, for example. The results reported by Rosenbaum (1992) may also be sensitive to attrition from the sample. For example, it might be the case that the children who could not be relocated in the suburbs had returned to the inner city.

Still, this is one instance in which an experimental approach promises to do an excellent job of severing the connection between neighborhood and family characteristics that makes it so difficult to draw inferences from survey data. HUD is currently planning several new experimental evaluations of voucher programs based on the Gautreaux model. It is hoped that these studies will provide more conclusive evidence about the potential costs and benefits of relocating low-income families.[57]

C. The Role of Housing Assistance Programs: The Construction of Public Housing Vs. Vouchers

Until 1974, housing assistance was provided almost exclusively through the production of subsidized housing. Since then, vouchers have become increasingly important. The rationale for this shift in policy is that it is cheaper to house a family in an existing unit under a voucher program than it is to build new public housing units (Apgar, 1990). Hence, more families can be served for the same budget outlay.

Apgar (1990) points out that subsidies will not always have a cost advantage. There are several issues that must be considered. First, it is possible that the provision of public housing could reduce rents on other low-rent housing by increasing the supply. However, according to Struyk (1990), vacancy rates for units below the FMR averaged at least 7% in most markets during the 80s. At these vacancy rates, increasing the supply is unlikely to lower rents.

On the other hand, it is sometimes argued that voucher payments could drive up rents by increasing demand for housing. This would raise serious equity issues since housing assistance is not available to all families. Hence, if rents are driven up, housing assistance will benefit some poor families at the expense of others.

Evidence from the Experimental Housing Allowance Program (EHAP), a series of controlled housing experiments conducted in the mid-70s, suggests that most households increase housing expenditures very little in response to subsidies (cf. Allen, Fitts and Grant (1981), Lowry (1983), Struyk and Bendick (1981), Rosen (1985), and Bradbury and Downs (1981)). Treatment families in these experiments received a payment equal to the gap between 25% of their income and 'the cost of standard housing'. Payments were made only to families living in housing meeting minimum standards, and these minimums varied both within and between experiments.

---

[57] Personal communication with Dr. Susan Mayer, Dept. of Sociology, University of Chicago.

In general, the experimental treatments had relatively small effects on the housing expenditures of eligible households, or on market rents. For example, 3 years after the experiments began in Green Bay, Wisconsin and South Bend, Illinois, RAND researchers found that half of the eligible families were not participating, that participating renters had increased their rental payments by only 8%, and that market rents had increased by only 2 to 3% (Rydell, Neels and Barnett, 1982). In a Pittsburgh experiment, renters subject to minimal housing standards spent only 6% of their subsidy on housing, while those subject to stricter minimum housing standards spent 9%. Higher estimates were obtained in Phoenix where the comparable figures were 19% and 27%. Researchers also found that participation rates dropped precipitously as housing standards were raised.

These small responses may reflect the fact that there are large transactions costs associated with moving, so households are hesitant to move in response to a temporary program. On average, the EHAP increased mobility among participating households by only 7 to 10% (Allen, Fitts, and Grant, 1981). Households that didn't have to move in order to meet the housing quality standards participated at twice the rate of other households. Landlords may also have been reluctant to participate in an unfamiliar experiment.

Apgar (1990) argues that a contemporary voucher program is likely to have larger effects both in terms of the participation of eligibles and the amount of the subsidy that is spent on housing. First, vouchers are now a familiar and apparently permanent feature of federal housing policy. Second, the cost of standard housing has risen as a share of participant income. Data from the 1986 Freestanding Voucher Demonstration program indicates that 60% of eligible households participated and that 57% of the subsidy went towards increasing rental payments (Kennedy and Finkel, 1987). No evidence is available about the effects of this program on the general level of rents. Still, the vacancy rates cited above suggest that new construction would relieve upward pressure on rents only in very tight housing markets.

Another issue that has been raised with respect to the provision of public housing, is whether public housing construction displaces the private construction of low-rent housing. Murray (1983) found that for every 100 units constructed, 75 units were net new additions to the stock of housing. But it has been argued that these results apply only to the large public housing projects he studied and not to the construction of small-scale units scattered throughout urban areas that has been favored in recent years (Struyk, 1990).

These discussions about the effects of housing policy on the quantity and price of assisted housing do not usually take direct account of the fact that many public housing projects have become 'bywards for despair' (Weicher, 1990). Twenty years ago, Henry Aaron wrote that 'Over the years public housing has acquired a vile image – highrise concrete monoliths in great impersonal cities, cut off from surrounding neighborhoods by grass or cement deserts best avoided after dark... This image suggests that any benefits inhabitants derive from physical housing amenities are offset by the squalid surroundings' (Aaron, 1972 p. 108).

This public image does not reflect the heterogeneity of housing projects, and is belied by the extremely long waiting lists described above. Still, many projects suffer from severe problems. A 1988 HUD study found that more than half of public housing households lived in projects that needed moderate to substantial rehabilitation just to meet HUD's own standards. The costs of bringing these units up to standard would exceed $20 billion 1986 dollars (Lazere *et al.*, 1991).

And the social consequences of isolating poor people in large projects are clear. It is unlikely that a 'market equivalent' rent that takes account of these conditions can be computed, since there are likely to be few market accommodations that have all the disamenities of large public housing projects. Hence, attempts to compare the cost of providing housing under voucher programs to the cost of building public housing may understate the cost advantage of the voucher programs by neglecting to adequately control for neighborhood quality.

On the other hand, the advantages of voucher programs should not be oversold. The Gautreaux program placed families in apartments located by the program. In contrast, many other housing authorities require families to locate a landlord willing to participate in the Section 8 program, and to arrange with the landlord for inspections and repairs. The unit usually needs to be located and occupied within a fixed period of time. One case study of 56 single mothers in eastern Massachusetts in 1985 and 1986 found that after waiting an average of 2 years to receive a certificate, 24 women returned them unused because they were unable to find housing that met program requirements within the allotted time (Mulroy, 1988). In addition, Johnson (1986), found that while recipients of housing allowances frequently move to better neighborhoods, they did not usually move to less segregated ones. These findings suggest that stricter enforcement of the 'fair housing provisions' of Civil Rights Act might enhance the effectiveness of voucher programs.

D. Summary

Despite the fact that housing constitutes the single largest expenditure of most families, little is known about the effects of housing on child health and well-being. And although the subject has been much researched, the effects of neighborhoods and schools on children's prospects remain controversial. However, the available evidence does suggest that a dollar spent on voucher programs is likely to have a more positive impact than a dollar spent on the construction of new public housing. Gautreaux-type experiments promise to provide important information about all these questions.

10. THE EARNED INCOME TAX CREDIT

The Earned Income Tax Credit is one of the most rapidly growing federal transfer programs. Yet, because it is administered through the tax system, it is not usually thought of as welfare. However, as we saw in Chapter 3, most spending is on the refundable portion of the credit, that is, on cash transfers to people whose tax liabilities are less than the value of their credits.

Although until OBRA'93 the EITC was available only to families with children, no research has been conducted regarding the effects of the credit on child well-being. It is difficult in principle to identify the effects of the EITC since the amount of the credit depends on the amount that parents work, a decision that is likely to be correlated with many factors relevant to child well-being. However, the EITC is in many respects similar to the 'Negative Income Tax' (NIT), an income guarantee program that was subjected to exhaustive scrutiny through a number of large-scale social experiments, although it was never implemented. This chapter draws the parallels between the two programs, and discusses what can be learned about the effects of cash transfers on child well-being from the NIT experiments.

A. Parallels Between the EITC and the NIT

i) How a NIT Works

The way a NIT works is illustrated in Figure 13. In the absence of the program the family's budget constraint is given by the line AD. Under a NIT, a family that earns no income is guaranteed a minimum level of income, Y_g. Families with earnings, Y_b, receive a payment D, where $D = Y_g - t_1 Y$. The quantity $Y_b = y_g / t_1$ is referred to as the breakeven level of

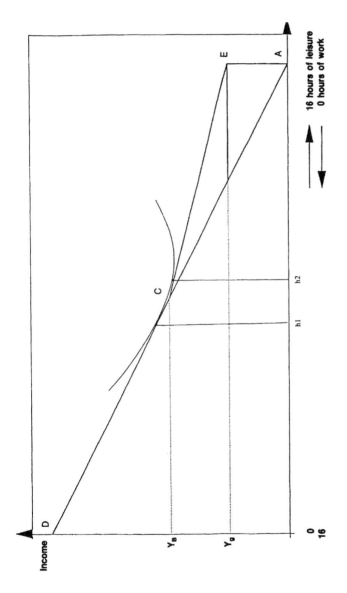

FIGURE 13   Budget constraint with a "Negative Income Tax".

income since workers who earn more than Y_b receive no payments. The new budget constraint for the family is given by the line ECD. If income is equal to the wage multiplied by hours worked, and workers face a tax rate t, then workers on the NIT earn (w-t-t_1) for every hour of work, whereas workers with incomes above Y_b earn (w-t). That is, workers on the NIT face a higher implicit tax rate than other workers, which is shown in the diagram by the fact that the line segment EC is 'flatter' than the segment AC.

This program was very popular among economists for several reasons. First, it was proposed that the NIT could be operated more efficiently than the existing welfare system with its patchwork of programs. Second, the NIT would reduce incentives for lone parenthood because it would be available to all families. Finally, the NIT would eliminate some of the work disincentive associated with programs like AFDC, by allowing work to be rewarded.

It is important to note that it would not eliminate all of the disincentive, however. The indifference curve in Figure 13 shows that a taxpayer who in the absence of the program would work h_1 hours and earn an income above the breakeven level might decide to cut back hours to h_2 and consume more leisure under the NIT. For people below the breakeven, the NIT both increases income and reduces the effective wage, so that both the income and substitution effects will encourage the consumption of leisure.

In order to investigate whether these work disincentives posed a serious threat to the validity of the NIT, the Office of Economic Opportunity under President Nixon authorized 4 large-scale social experiments. The first experiment, in New Jersey and Pennsylvania, lasted from 1968 until 1972 and involved 1,357 low-income couples. A rural experiment took place in Iowa and North Carolina from 1969 to 1973 and included 809 low-income rural families. A third experiment was conducted in Gary, Indiana between 1971 and 1974 and was composed of 1,780 African-American households, 59% of them female-headed. The largest experiment, which affected 4,800 families, was conducted in Seattle and Denver from 1971 to 1982.

The NIT experiments were the first large-scale attempt to investigate social policy using a treatment and control design. Treatments consisted of assigning a guarantee level and a tax rate. The guarantees were usually expressed as a percent of the federal poverty line, and ranged from 50 to 250%. The average payments in the Seattle/Denver experiment, for example, ranged from $919 to $2031 (1972 dollars) depending on the treatment group. By way of comparison, the maximum AFDC benefit for a family of 3 in 1970 was $2,316 in Colorado and $2,208 in Oregon, and the poverty line for a family of 3 persons was $3,099.

Unfortunately, the designers of the experiments ran into many of the pitfalls discussed in Chapter 1. One major problem is that in order to save money subjects with lower incomes were placed in less generous treatments. This means that treatments and controls were randomized only within income brackets so that in many cases the cell-sizes available for comparisons of treatments and controls are very small (Ashenfelter and Plant, 1990). A second problem is that in some states the welfare system changed during the period of the experiment and caused many controls to drop out. These problems mean that analysts have had to resort to non-experimental techniques in order to analyze the experimental data.

ii) *How the EITC Works*

The workings of the EITC are illustrated in Table 25. The figures in the table are taken from the 1991 tax schedule and apply to families with 1 child who take the standard deductions. For simplicity, it is assumed that households have no asset income. The table shows that both the EITC and tax liabilities increase with earnings. For workers with very low earnings, the credit exceeds tax liabilities so that they receive a cash transfer. For families with earnings above $11,920, the EITC begins to be phased out so that it offsets less and less of the family's increasing tax liabilities. The net

TABLE 25
The Interaction of the EITC and the Tax System in 1991
(Family with one Qualifying Child and only Standard Deductions)

Earnings	EITC	Tax		Refundable credit		Net income	
		Married	Single	Married	Single	Married	Single
4,000	672	0	0	672	672	4,672	4,672
5,000	839	0	0	839	839	5,839	5,839
6,000	1,006	0	0	1,006	1,006	7,006	7,006
7,000	1,173	0	0	1,173	1,073	8,173	8,173
8,000	1,192	0	0	1,192	1,192	9,192	9,192
9,000	1,192	0	0	1,192	1,192	10,192	10,192
10,000	1,192	0	107	1,192	1,085	11,192	11,085
11,000	1,192	148	253	1,044	939	12,044	11,939
13,000	981	746	559	533	422	13,533	13,422
15,000	742	1,504	851	0	0	14,996	14,891
20,000	146	1,504	1,609	0	0	18,642	18,537

Note: Married couples are assumed to file jointly. Single refers to a single household head.

result is to flatten the income profile by raising the after-tax incomes of households with very low earnings and lowering the incomes of households with somewhat higher earnings.

Both the EITC and the NIT work through the tax system to increase the level and reduce the variance of income among the poor. However, the EITC differs from the NIT because it lowers effective marginal tax rates for the poorest rather than raising them. On the other hand, recipients in the 'phase out' range of the EITC face work disincentives very similar to those faced by NIT participants.

OBRA'93 embodies President Clinton's pledge to expand the EITC in order "to guarantee a 'working wage' so that no American who works full-time is forced to raise children in poverty" (Clinton and Gore, 1992). This guarantee differs in spirit from the NIT guarantee since it is conditional on working full-time.

B . Effects of the NIT

Most research on the NIT focuses on the question of work disincentives. The consensus is that the effects were in the direction predicted by economic theory: treatments tended to reduce their work hours relative to controls, and the effects were greater for women (who presumably had more attractive non-market opportunities) than for men. However, the labor supply effects were small in magnitude. There has been some speculation about whether a permanent NIT program might induce larger behavioral responses. This question of whether subjects viewed NIT payments as transitory or permanent additions to income should be kept in mind when reviewing the non-labor supply responses to the NIT discussed in the rest of this section.

i) Effects on Family Stability

There are several reasons why one might expect a NIT to affect the stability of families. First, the NIT removes some of the marriage disincentives inherent in the AFDC program by offering benefits to both intact and single-parent families. On the other hand, like AFDC, the NIT offers support to parents outside of marriage and so may increase the incidence of marital dissolution and of extra-marital child-bearing. Given that children in single-parent households are at higher risk of poverty than other children, evidence that a program encouraged marital dissolution would have to be taken very seriously.

It is not surprising then that one of the most sensational findings of the NIT experiments was that treatments tended to suffer more marital dissolutions than controls. In their examination of the first three years of data from the Seattle/Denver experiment, Groeneveld, Hannan and Tuma (1980) found that the overall rate at which marriages dissolved increased by 40% to 60%. However, the rate was highest for couples in the least generous plans, while the most generous plans had no adverse impact on marital stability. It is difficult to interpret this result because, as noted above, couples were not randomly assigned to plans: higher income couples were more likely to be assigned to a generous plan. Hence, a possible interpretation is that the independence offered by the NIT was more attractive to lower-income than to higher-income women.

These findings have been challenged by Cain and Wissoker (1990) who find that when couples without children are excluded from the sample, and all available years of Seattle/Denver data are examined,[58] the effects of the experimental treatments are not statistically significant. In a reply, Hannan and Tuma (1990) argue that the full set of estimates from both studies suggest a positive effect of the NIT on the probability of marital dissolution, although the point estimates are not precisely estimated.

ii) *Effects on Health*

Kehrer and Wolin (1979) analyzed data on 404 single live births to participants in the Gary experiment. Mean birthweight for treatment infants was 3147 grams compared to 3173 grams for the control infants which suggests that the NIT had little impact on mean birthweight. Nor do they find any differences in the number of prenatal care visits or in the month that prenatal care began. These results are similar to those of Currie and Cole (1993) in that income transfers appear to have had little effect on the utilization of prenatal care or on birthweight.

Lefcowitz and Elesh (1977) examine the effects of the New Jersey experiment on the health care utilization of children. The measures they examine include the numbers of chronic illnesses, hospital stays, bed days, and doctor visits. Once again they find virtually no effect of the NIT treatments.

---

[58] The analysis of the Seattle/Denver data is complicated by the fact that some households were in 3-year experiments while others were enrolled in 5-year experiments.

136   JANET CURRIE

TABLE 26
School Performance in the Rural Experiment
Differences between Treatments and Controls
as a Percent of Control Mean

Measure	Grades 2-8 North Carolina	Iowa	Grades 9-12 North Carolina	Iowa
Days absent	-30**	-20	3	-17
Comportment	7**	0	n.e.	n.e.
Academic Grades	6*	-5	4	-5
Achievement Tests (deviation from norm)	19**	-18.8	n.e.	n.e.

Source: Maynard and Crawford (1976). There were 847 children.
  * Significant at the 90% level of confidence.
  ** Significant at the 95% level of confidence.
  n.e. Not estimated due to lack of data.

O'Conner, Madden, and Pringle (1976), examined the effect of the NIT on nutrition in the rural experiment. Using 24-hour dietary recall, they examined the intakes of 10 nutrients in the third and eleventh quarters of the experiment. Among subjects in North Carolina, they found positive and significant treatment effects on intakes of energy, calcium, phosphorus, iron, riboflavin and vitamin C. These effects are particularly noteworthy since before the experiment began, 60% of the North Carolina sample had inadequate calcium intakes, 50% had inadequate iron intakes and more than a third lacked vitamin C. However, the treatment did not appear to have a significant effect in Iowa, a finding that the authors attribute to the relative poverty of the North Carolina sample.

iii) Effects on Test Scores and Educational Attainment

The rural and Gary experiments collected information about school performance. The results from the rural experiment are summarized in Table 26. Elementary school children from NIT families in North Carolina showed significant improvements in attendance, comportment and achievement. However, there were no effects for older children or for elementary school children in Iowa. Maynard and Crawford (1976) attribute this pattern of results to the fact that the children in North Carolina were much more disadvantaged than those in Iowa.

Maynard and Murnane (1979) examined the school performance of the children in the Gary experiment. These children differed from children in the other experiments since all of them were African-American, and three-fifths of them lived in female-headed households. They found that the NIT treatment had positive effects on the reading scores of younger children and that these effects were significant for children whose families had been in the program for 3 or more years.

In an analysis of data from the New Jersey experiment, Mallar (1977) found that teenagers whose parents were enrolled in a NIT plan were between 20% and 90% more likely to complete high school depending on the parameters of the plan. This group also completed one-third to one-and-a-half more years of education than their counterparts in the control group. However, Venti (1984) found an 11% increase in the probability of completing high school for youth in the Seattle/Denver experiment. This lower estimate seems more probable in view of the relatively short duration of the experiments, and the many long-term factors (such as achievement in early grades) that have been linked to educational attainment.

iv) Effects on Housing

One of the most striking findings of the NIT experiments is that families tended to upgrade their housing. Treatments in the Gary and Seattle/Denver experiments were more likely than controls to become first-time homebuyers. For example, Pozdena and Johnson (1980) found that female-headed households in the Seattle/Denver experiment were 50% more likely to buy a home and that they increased their mortgage debt by nearly 40%. The evidence from the New Jersey experiment is more controversial: Wooldridge (1977) finds that treatment families above the breakeven were more likely than control families to buy homes. She interprets this as evidence that stabilizing income can have an effect independent of the level of payments. However Poirier (1977) finds that some of this effect is actually due to mobility: when he limits the sample to those who changed their housing, he finds that the treatment only had an effect on the probability of homeownership among African-Americans.

Wooldridge also finds that treatment families who rented increased their rental payments relative to controls. These increases were related to guarantee levels: those in the most generous treatments increased their rents by 25% per month, while those in the least generous averaged increases of only 6%. Treatments were also significantly more likely to move out of public housing than controls. Specifically, a 25% increase in the generosity of the guarantee was associated with a 4% decrease in the probability of living in public housing. Avrin (1980) obtained similar estimates of the effect of the NIT on the probability that a female-headed household lived in public housing using data from the Seattle/Denver experiment.

C. Summary

The NIT experiments provide the only solid evidence we have that transfers to parents have measurable positive effects on children. Transfers to the poorest families appear to improve children's school performance and nutritional status. Families also upgrade their housing in response to transfers - a change that may have a large impact on children's lives.

In the end, the NIT turned out to be politically unacceptable because it created the same sort of undesirable incentives as AFDC: income guarantees and high tax rates diminish the returns to work, and may provide an incentive for lone parents to become heads of household.

The political success of the EITC may be due to the fact that by eliminating the income guarantee, decreasing marginal tax rates for the poorest, and making the transfer conditional on work, the program provides work incentives and transfers to the poorest working parents.

CONCLUSIONS

Economists have long argued that in-kind transfer programs are an inefficient way to increase the well-being of welfare recipients. We have seen for example, that families increase food purchases less than a quarter in response to a dollar increase in food stamp benefits, and that they spend at most half of a dollar's worth of housing vouchers on rents. Since families on welfare clearly prefer to buy a different basket of goods than the one that government wishes to provide, wouldn't their well-being be maximized by giving them the money and allowing them to choose for themselves? Forcing people to consume goods they don't want wastes scarce resources. And the fact that new bureaucracies must be created to administer each type of in-kind benefits creates additional inefficiencies.

The logic of these arguments notwithstanding, the proportion of assistance provided in-kind has grown steadily in the past 15 years, and the programs that are growing fastest are those that are the most restrictive in terms of the kinds of benefits offered. The answer to this paradox is that welfare is not intended to benefit all recipients equally. Americans are concerned about the plight of children in poor families, but reluctant to aid able-bodied adults.

Hence the popularity of programs that provide specific benefits directly to children.

And these programs deliver: children on Medicaid are more likely to receive routine checkups than similar children; WIC has a positive impact on birthweight and child nutrition; and participation in Head Start leads to at least short-term and possibly longer term gains in cognitive functioning and schooling attainment.[59]

Moreover, the more targeted the program, the larger the measurable effect seems to be. For example, the Food Stamp Program is the in-kind program that most resembles a cash transfer in terms of fungibility and it has the least well-documented effects. The effects of housing assistance are similarly difficult to pin down, although the Gautreaux experiments suggest that a voucher program that enabled families to find homes in good neighborhoods could significantly improve the life chances of children. A comparison of the School Lunch Program with the School Breakfast Program also suggests that programs with stricter federal guidelines are likely to have larger effects.

In contrast, it is very difficult to identify any positive effect of cash transfers under the AFDC program. This does not mean that there are no benefits. Evidence from the Negative Income Tax experiments suggests that among the poorest families, cash transfers can have a positive impact on child nutrition and schooling attainment. However, payments under the NIT program were in the range of one-third to two-thirds of the poverty line, which was $10,522 for a family with one adult and two children in 1990. It would have required a payment of $4,000 to bring this family up to the poverty line, assuming that the adult worked full time at $5.00 per hour. This back-of-the-envelope calculation suggests that it requires a relatively large cash transfer to generate any measurable benefit. Moreover, despite evidence that the labor supply effects are small, the public believes that cash transfers under the AFDC program are used to subsidize the leisure of adults.

The EITC is less subject to this criticism because the size of the transfer depends on the parent's earnings. However, for this very reason, it is unlikely to ever provide a complete substitute for the present welfare system. It seems then that we are moving towards a two-tiered system in which families without bread-winners receive most of their benefits in-kind, while

---

[59] One caveat is that if these programs now serve only the neediest, their average impact may be smaller if they are extended to all eligible children.

the 'working poor' receive cash transfers. Whether this is a desirable development depends on one's point of view. On the one hand, although it is difficult to value the benefits, programs that provide in-kind transfers directly to children have demonstrable effects. But the assumption underlying a system of in-kind transfers is that the 'non-working poor' cannot be trusted to do what is best for their own children.

Many people will find the assumption that 'the government knows best' disturbing and paternalistic. It is worth pointing out in this regard that the provision of in-kind benefits is a relatively innocuous exercise of state power compared to other recent attempts to modify family structure and parenting behavior through the welfare system. New Jersey and California plan to deny benefits to children conceived on AFDC; several states continue to try to force teenaged mothers to live with their parents; and Wisconsin has attempted to withhold the benefits of AFDC families whose children do not attend school. Maryland has considered cutting AFDC benefits 30% if children do not attend school or if parents do not have them immunized (Smolensky et al., 1992). And it was not until the late '60s and early '70s that systematic harassment of welfare recipients and the arbitrary denial of benefits were first challenged in the courts (Sard, 1988).

It seems clear that the worst case scenario for children dependent on welfare is the continuing erosion of cash AFDC benefits without concomitant increases in in-kind benefits. The results surveyed here suggest that the trend towards increasing the proportion of assistance proffered in-kind is likely to benefit children, although it raises unresolved issues regarding parents' rights.

REFERENCES

Aaron, Henry. *Shelter and Subsidies: Who Benefits From Federal Housing Policies?*, Washington D.C.: Brookings Institution, 1972.
Adams, KE. 'Effect of Increased Medicaid Fees on Physician Participation in Tennessee, 1985–1988', Washington D.C.: Systemetrics, April 1992.
Aday, Lu Ann. 'Health Insurance and Utilization of Medical Care for Chronically Ill Children with Special Needs', Advance data from Vital and Health Statistics # 215, Hyattsville MD: National Center for Health Statistics, 1992.
Alan Guttmacher Institute, *The Financing of Maternity Care in the United States*, New York, 1988.
Allen, Garland, Jerry Fitts and Evelyn Grant. 'The Experimental Housing Allowance Program,' in Katharine Bradbury and Anthony Downs (eds.) *Do Housing Allowances Work?*, Washington D.C.: The Brookings Institution, 1981.
Altonji, Joseph. 'The Effect of High School Curriculum on Education and Labor Market Outcomes,' National Bureau of Economic Research Working Paper #4142, August 1992.

Altonji, Joseph. 'The Effects of Family Background and School Characteristics on Education and Labor Market Outcomes,' mimeo, Department of Economics Northwestern University, December, 1988.

Antel, John. 'The Inter-Generational Transfer of Welfare Dependency', University of Houston, mimeo, 1989.

Apgar, William. "Which Housing Policy is Best?" *Housing Policy Debate,* **1 #1**, 1990, 1–32.

Ashenfelter, Orley and Mark Plant. 'Nonparametric Estimates of the Labor Supply Effects of Negative Income Tax Programs', *Journal of Labor Economics,* **8 #1**, 396–415, January 1990.

Ashenfelter, Orley, Janet Currie, Henry Farber, and Matthew Spiegel. 'An Experimental Comparison of Dispute Rates in Alternative Arbitration Systems', *Econometrica,* **60 #6**, November 1992, 1407–1434.

Ashenfelter, Orley. 'Determining Participation in Income Tested Social Programs', *Journal of the American Statistical Association,* September 1983.

Avrin, Marcy. 'Utilization of Subsidized Housing,' in *A Guaranteed Annual Income: Evidence from a Social Experiment,* New York: Academic Press, 1980.

Baker, Paula and Frank Mott. *NLSY Child Handbook, 1989,* Center for Human Resource Research, The Ohio State University, Columbus Ohio, June 1989.

Becker, Gary. 'Family Economics and Macro Behavior', *The American Economic Review,* **78**, 1–13, March 1988.

Bee, C.K. 'A Longitudinal Study to Determine if Head Start has Lasting Effects on School Achievement,' *Dissertation Abstracts International,* **42(5)**, 1981.

Beebout, Harold, Edward Cavin, Barbara Devaney *et al.* '*Evaluation of the Nutrition Assistance Program in Puerto Rico, Volume II – Effects on Food Expenditures and Diet Quality,'* Washington D.C.: USDA Food and Nutrition Service, 1985.

Behman, Jere and Paul Taubman. 'Intergenerational Earnings Mobility in the United States', *Review of Economics and Statistics,* **67**, 144–51, February 1985.

Berrueta-Clement, J.R. *et al.* 'Changed Lives: The Effects of the Perry Preschool Program on Youths Through Age 19,' Ypsilanti, MI: High Scope (1985).

Birch, Herbert and Joan Gussow. *Disadvantaged Children, Health, Nutrition, and School Failure,* New York: Harcourt, Brace, and World, 1970.

Blanchard, Lois, *et al. Food Stamp SSI/Elderly Cashout Demonstration Evaluation,* Washington D.C.: USDA Food and Nutrition Service, 1982.

Blank, Rebecca. 'The Effect of Medical Need and Medicaid on AFDC Participation,' *The Journal of Human Resources,* **24 #1**, Winter 1989, 54–87.

Blank, Rebecca and Patricia Ruggles. 'When Do Women use AFDC and Food Stamps? The Dynamics of Eligibility vs. Participation,' NBER Working Paper #4429, August 1993.

Blau, Francine and Adam Grossberg. 'Maternal Labor Supply and Children's Cognitive Development', National Bureau of Economic Research Working Paper #3536, Dec. 1990.

Bloom, Barbara. 'Health Insurance and Medical Care', *Advance Data from Vital and Health Statistics of the National Center for Health Statistics,* #188, Public Health Service, Washington D.C., October 1, 1990.

Borden, Enid and Kate O'Beirne. 'False Start? The Fleeting Gains at Head Start,' *Policy Review,* Winter 1989.

Bound, John, David Jaeger and Regina Baker. 'The Cure Can be Worse than the Disease: A Cautionary Tale Regarding Instrumental Variables', University of Michigan at Ann Arbor, mimeo, February 1993.

Bowden, Roger and Darrell Turkington. *Instrumental Variables,* New York: Cambridge University Press, 1984.

Bradbury, Katharine and Anthony Downs (eds.) *Do Housing Allowances Work?,* Washington D.C.: The Brookings Institution, 1981.

Bronfenbrenner, U. 'Is Early Intervention Effective?' in M. Guttentag and E. Stuening (eds.) *Handbook of Evaluation Research*, v.2, 519-603, Beverly Hills: Sage. 1975.

Brooks-Gunn, J. and F.F. Furstenberg. 'The Children of Adolescent Mothers: Physical, Academic, and Psychological Outcomes', *Developmental Review,* **6**. 1986, 224–251.

Buescher *et al.* 'An Evaluation of the Impact of Maternity Care Coordination on Medicaid Birth Outcomes in North Carolina', *American Journal of Public Health*, **81**, 1991, 1625–1629.

Butler, J.S., James Ohls, and Barbara Posner. 'The Effect of the Food Stamp Program on the Nutrient Intake of the Eligible Elderly', *The Journal of Human Resources*, **20**, 1985, 405-420.

Butler, J.A., E.D. Winter, J.D. Singer, *et al.* 'Medical Care Use and Expenditure Among Children and Youth in the United States: Analysis of a National Probability Sample,' *Pediatrics*, **76**, 1985, 495–507.

Caan, Bette, Donna Horgen, Sheldon Margen *et al.* 'Benefits Associated with WIC Supplemental Feeding During the Interpregnancy Interval,' *The American Journal of Clinical Nutrition*, **45**, 1987, 29–41.

Cain, Glen and Douglas Wissoker. 'A Reanalysis of Marital Stability in the Seattle-Denver Income-Maintenance Experiment,' *American Journal of Sociology*, **95 #5**, March 1990, 1235–69.

Center for Health Statistics. *Advance Report of Final Natality Statistics*, Monthly Vital Statistics Report, v 40 # 8, Department of Health and Human Services, Hyattsville, MD, 1991.

Center for Population Options. *Teenage Pregnancy and Too-Early Childbearing: Public Costs, Personal Consequences*, Washington D.C., 1990.

Chandra, R. 'Nutritional and Immunity-Basic Considerations', *Contemporary Nutrition*, **II**, 1986.

Chavas, Jean-Paul and M.L. Yeung. 'Effects of the Food Stamp Program on Food Consumption in the Southern United States,' *Southern Journal of Agricultural Economics*, July 1982, 131–139.

Chen, Jain-Shing. *Simultaneous Equations Models with Qualitative Dependent Variables: Food Stamp Program Participation and Food Cost Analysis*, Ph.D. dissertation, University of Missouri, 1983.

Clark, R. and J. Menefee. 'Federal Expenditures for the Elderly: Past and Future,' *The Gerontologist*, April 1981.

Clarkson, Kenneth. *Food Stamps and Nutrition*, Washington D.C.: American Enterprise Institute, 1975.

Cleveland, W.S. 'Robust Locally-Weighted Regressions and Smoothing Scatterplots,' *Journal of the American Statistical Association*, **74**, 1979, 829–836.

Clinton, William and Albert Gore; *Putting People First*, New York: Times Books, 1992.

Coburn, Andrew F. and Thomas P. McDonald. 'The Effects of Variations in AFDC and Medicaid Eligibility on Prenatal Care Use,' *Social Science and Medicine*, **35#8**, Oct. 92, 1055–63.

Coder, John, Lee Rainwater, and Timothy Smeeding. 'Inequality Among Children and Elderly in Ten Modern Nations: The United States in an International Context', *The American Economic Review,* **v79 #2**, May 1989, 320–324.

Coe, Richard. 'Nonparticipation in Welfare Programs by Eligible Households: The Case of the Food Stamp Program,' *Journal of Economic Issues*, **XVII 4**, December 1983, 1035-1057.

Colle, Ann and Michael Grossman. 'Determinants of Pediatric Care Utilization', *The Journal of Human Resources*, **XIII**, 1978, 115-158.

Commerce Clearing House. *Medicare and Medicaid Guide*, New York: Commerce Clearing House, 1987.

Consortium for Longitudinal Studies. *As the Twig is Bent: Lasting Effects of Preschool Programs,* Hillsdale, NJ:Erlbaum, 1983.

Copple, C.E. Cline, M.G., and Smith, A.N. *Path to the Future: Long-Term Effects of Head Start in the Philadelphia School District,* Washington D.C.: Head Start Bureau, U.S. Department of Health and Human Services, 1987.

Corbett, Thomas. 'Child Poverty and Welfare Reform: Progress or Paralysis?, *Focus,* **15 #1,** Spring 1993, 1-17.

Corcoran, Mary *et al.* 'Effects of Family and Community Background on Men's Economic Status', National Bureau of Economic Research Working Paper # 2896, March 1989.

Cramer, James. 'Explaining Demographic Differences in Low Birth Weight and Infant Mortality', final research report, Center for Population Research, National Institute of Child Health and Human Development, 1987.

Crane, Jonathan. 'Effects of Neighborhoods on Dropping Out of School and Teenage Childbearing, in *The Urban Underclass,* Christopher Jencks and Paul Peterson (eds.), Washington D.C.: The Brookings Institution, 1991.

Currie, Janet and Duncan Thomas. 'Medical Care for Children: Public Insurance, Private Insurance, and Racial Differences in Utilization,' *Journal of Human Resources,* forthcoming, 1995.

Currie, Janet and Duncan Thomas. 'Does Head Start Make a Difference?' University of California at Los Angeles, mimeo, May 1993b.

Currie, Janet and Nancy Cole. 'Does Participation in Transfer Programs During Pregnancy Improve Birth Weight?' National Bureau of Economic Research Working Paper # **3832,** Sept. 1991.

Currie, Janet and Nancy Cole. 'Welfare and Child Health: The Link Between AFDC Participation and Birth Weight', *The American Economic Review,* **283 #3,** 1993.

Currie, Janet and Jonathan Gruber. 'Saving Babies: The Efficacy and Cost of Recent Expansions of Medicaid Eligibility for Pregnant Women,' National Bureau of Economic Research, mimeo, December 1993.

Danzinger, Sheldon and Jonathan Stern. 'The Causes amd Consequences of Child Poverty in the United States', Population Studies Center, University of Michigan, Research Report No. 90-194, September 1990.

Datta, L. 'Another Spring and Other Hopes: Some Findings From National Evaluations of Project Head Start,' in E. Zigler and J. Valentine (eds.), *Project Head Start: A Legacy of the War on Poverty,* 405–432, New York: Free Press, 1979.

Davis, Karen and R. Reynolds. 'The Impact of Medicare and Medicaid on Access to Medical Care,' in R.N. Rosette ed., *The Role of Health Insurance in the Health Services Sector* (National Bureau of Economic Research, New York, NY), 1976, 391–435.

Decker, Sandra. 'The Effect of Physician Reimbursement Levels on the Primary Care of Medicaid Patients', PhD. thesis, Harvard University, 1993.

Desai, Sonalde, P.L. Chase-Lansdale and Robert Michael. 'Mother or Market? Effects of Maternal Employment on the Intellectual Ability of 4-year-old Children', *Demography,* **26 #4,** November 1989, 545-561.

Devaney, Barbara and Thomas Fraker. 'Cashing Out Food Stamps: Impacts on Food Expenditures and Diet Quality,' *Journal of Policy Analysis and Management,* **5,** 1986, 725-741.

Devaney, Barbara, Linda Bilheimer, and Jennifer Schore. *The Savings in Medicaid Costs for Newborns and Their Mothers from Prenatal Participation in the WIC Program,* Mathematica Policy Research, Inc.: Washington D.C., October 1990.

Devaney, Barbara, Pamela Haines, and Robert Moffitt. *Assessing the Dietary Effects of the Food Stamp Program, Volume 1: Conceptual Design,* Mathematica Policy Research Project #7665-450 and 7665-710, February 14, 1989a.

Devaney, Barbara, Pamela Haines, and Robert Moffitt. *Assessing the Dietary Effects of the Food Stamp Program, Volume 2: Empirical Results*, Mathematica Policy Research Project #7665-450 and 7665-710, February 14, 1989b.

Devaney, Barbara, and Alan Schirm. *Infant Mortality Among Medicaid Newborns in Five States: The Effects of Prenatal WIC Participation*, Washington D.C.: U.S. Dept. of Agriculture, Food and Nutrition Service, May 1993.

Deaton, Angus and John Muellbauer. 'On Measuring Child Costs: With Applications to Poor Countries,' *Journal of Political Economy*, **94 #4**, August 1986, 720-744.

Dolbeare, Cushing: *Federal Housing Assistance: Who Needs It? Who Gets It?*, Washington D.C.: The National League of Cities, 1985.

Dolbeare, Cushing. *The Widening Gap, Housing Needs of Low Income Families*, Washington D.C.: Low Income Housing Information Service, June 1992.

Duncan, Greg and Saul Hoffman. 'Welfare Benefits, Economic Opportunities, and Out-of-Wedlock Births Among Black Teenage Girls', *Demography*, **27 #4**, November 1990, 519-535.

Eberstadt, Nicholas, 'America's Infant Mortality Puzzle', *The Public Interest*, 1991, 30-47.

Edelman, Marian Wright. *Families in Peril*, Cambridge MA: Harvard University Press, 1987.

Edin, Kathryn. 'Surviving the Welfare System: How AFDC Recipients Make Ends Meet in Chicago,' in *Social Problems*, **38 #4**, November 1991, 462-474.

Edozien, Joseph, Boyd Switzer and Rebecca Bryan. 'Medical Evaluation of the Special Supplemental Food Program for Women, Infants and Children.' *The American Journal of Clinical Nutrition*, **32**, March 1979.

Eissa, Nada and Jeffery Leibman. 'The End of Welfare As We Know It? Behavioral Responses to the Earned Income Tax Credit,' Dept. of Economics, Harvard University, mimeo, January 1994.

Ellwood, David. *Poor Support*, New York: Basic Books, 1988.

Ellwood, David and Mary Jo Bane. 'The Impact of AFDC on Family Structure and Living Arrangements', in *Research in Labor Economics*, R. Ehrenberg (ed), 7, Greenwich: JAI Press, 1985, 137-207.

Ellwood, David. 'The Spacial Mismatch Hypothesis: Are There Teenage Jobs Missing in the Ghetto, in *The Black Youth Employment Crisis*, Richard Freeman and Harry Holzer (eds.), Chicago IL: University of Chicago Press, 1986.

Ensminger, Margaret and Anita Slusarcick. 'Paths to High School Graduation or Dropout: A Longitudinal Study of a First-Grade Cohort,' *Sociology of Education*, **65**, April 1992, 95-113.

Feinstein, Jonathan. 'The Relationship Between Socio-economic Status and Health: A Survey', National Bureau of Economic Research, mimio, March 1992.

Floud, Roderick, Kenneth Wachter and Annabel Gregory. *Height, Health, and History*, Cambridge University Press: Cambridge, 1990.

Fogel, Robert. 'Physical growth as a Measure of the Economic Well-being of Populations: The Eighteenth and Nineteenth Centuries', in *Human Growth: A Comprehensive Treatise*, F. Falkner and J. Tanner (eds.), v.3, 2nd Ed., New York: Plenum Press, 1986.

Food Research and Action Center, *Community Childhood Hunger Identification Project*, Washington, D.C.: FRAC, March 1991.

Forbes, D. and W.P. Frisbie. 'Spanish Surname and Anglo Infant Mortality: Differentials over a Half-Century', *Demography*, **28 #4**, 1991, 639-660.

Fossett, J.W., J. Perloff, P.R. Kletke, and J. Peterson. 'Medicaid and Access to Child Health Care in Chicago', *Journal of Health Politics, Policy, and Law*, 1993.

Fraker, Thomas. *The Effects of Food Stamps on Food Consumption: A Review of the Literature*, Washington D.C.: USDA Food and Nutrition Service, October 1990a.

Fraker, Thomas, Sharon Long, and Charles Post. *Analyses of the 1985 Continuing Survey of Food Intakes by Individuals, Volume 1 – Estimating Usual Dietary Intake, Assessing Adequacy and Estimating Program Effects*, Washington D.C.: USDA Food and Nutrition Service, 1990.

Fraker, Thomas. *Analyses of the 1985 Continuing Survey of Food Intakes by Individuals Volume II – Estimating the Effects of the WIC and Food Stamp Programs on Dietary Intake by Women and Young Children*, Washington D.C.: USDA Food and Nutrition Service, March 16, 1990b.

Garfinkel, Irwin and Sara McLanahan. *Single Mothers and Their Children*, Washington D.C.: The Urban Institute Press, 1986.

Garn and Clark. 'Nutrition, Growth, Development, and Maturation: Findings from a 10-State Nutrition Survey of 1968-1970,' *Pediatrics*, **56(2)**: 306-319, 1975.

Goodstein H.A., R.R. Cawley, and M.J. Burrows. 'The Prediction of Elementary School Failure Among High Risk Children,' Storrs CT: Connecticut University (ERIC Document Reproduction Service No. ED 108 749), 1975.

Gottschalk, Peter. 'Is the Correlation in Welfare Participation across Generations Spurious?' Boston College mimeo, January 1992.

Gottschalk, Peter. 'AFDC Participation Across Generations', *The American Economic Review*, **80 #2**, May 1990, 367-371.

Groeneveld, Lyle, Nancy Tuma and Michael Hannan. 'Marital Dissolution and Remarriage,' in *A Guaranteed Annual Income: Evidence from a Social Experiment*, Philip Robins, Robert Spiegelman, Samuel Weiner and Joseph Bell (eds), New York: Academic Press, 1980.

Grossman, Michael and Theodore Joyce. 'Unobservables, Pregnancy Resolutions, and Birth Weight Production Functions in New York City', *Journal of Political Economy*, **98**, October 1990, 983-1007.

Hannan, Michael and Nancy Tuma. 'A Reassessment of the Effect of Income Maintenance on Marital Dissolution in the Seattle-Denver Experiment,' *American Journal of Sociology*, **95 #5**, March 1990.

Hanes, S., J. Vermeersch, and S. Gale. 'The National Evaluation of School Nutrition Programs: Program Impact on Dietary Intake', *The American Journal of Clinical Nutrition*, **40**, August 1984, 390-413.

Hanratty, Maria and Rebecca Blank. 'Down and Out in North America: Recent Trends in Poverty Rates in the United States and Canada,' February 1992, 233-254.

Hanratty, Maria. 'Canadian National Health Insurance and Infant Health,' Dept. of Economics, Cornell University, mimeo, 1992.

Hardle, W. *Applied Nonparametric Regression*, New York: Cambridge University Press, 1990.

Harrington, Michael. *The Other America*, Baltimore: Penguin, 1962.

Haskins, Ronald. 'Beyond Metaphor: The Efficacy of Early Childhood Education,' *American Psychologist*, **44 2**, 274-282, Feb. 1989.

Hausman, Jerry and David Wise (eds.). *Social Experimentation*, Chicago: University of Chicago Press, 1985.

Haveman, Robert, Barbara Wolfe and James Spaulding. 'Childhood Events and Circumstances Influencing High School Completion,' *Demography*, **28 #1**, February 1991, 133-157.

Hayes, Cheryl, John Palmer, and Martha Zaslow. *Who Cares for America's Children: Child Care Policy for the 1990s*, Washington D.C.: National Academy Press, 1990.

Head Start Bureau, *Head Start Program Performance Standards*, U.S. Department of Health and Human Services Publication # ACF 92-31131, June 1992.

Hebbeler, K. 'An Old and a New Question on the Effects of Early Education for Children from Low Income Families,' *Educational Evaluation and Policy Analysis*, **7**, 207-216, 1985.

Heckman, James. 'Shadow Prices, Market Wages, and Labor Supply', *Econometrica*, **42**, 1974, 679-694.

Heckman, James and Joseph Hotz. 'Choosing Among Alternative Nonexperimental Methods
    for Estimating the Impact of Social Programs: The Case of Manpower Training Programs',
    Dept. of Economics, University of Chicago, mimeo, 1988.
Heckman, James and Thomas MaCurdy. 'A Simultaneous Equations Linear Probability Model',
    Canadian Journal of Economics, February 1985, 28-37.
Heckman, James. 'Sample Selection Bias as a Specification Error', Econometrica, 47, 1979,
    153-161.
Herbers, John. 'Hunger in U.S. Is Widening Study of 'New Poor' Reports'. New York Times,
    April 20 1986, 1.
Hicks, Lou, Rose Langham, and Jean Takenaka. 'Cognitive and Health Measures Following
    Early Nutritional Supplementation: A Sibling Study', American Journal of Public Health,
    72, 1982, 1110-1118.
Hill, M. and M. Ponza. 'Does Welfare Dependency Beget Dependency?' University of
    Michigan, mimeo, 1986.
Hill, Anne and June O'Neill. 'The Transmission of Cognitive Achievement Across Three
    Generations', Baruch College City, University of New York, mimeo, June 1992.
Hofferth, Sandra and C. Hayes (eds). Risking the Future, Washington: National Academy Press,
    1987.
Homer, Charles J., 'Evaluation of the Evidence on the Effectiveness of Well Child Care
    Services for Children', mimeo, Massachusetts General Hospital, July 21, 1988.
Horowitz, F.D. and Paden, L.Y. 'The Effectiveness of Environmental Intervention Programs,'
    in B. Caldwell and H. Ricciuti (eds.) Review of Child Developmental Research, v.3,
    331-402, Chicago: University of Chicago Press.
Hotz, Joseph. 'Recent Experiences in Designing Evaluations of Social Programs: The Case of
    the National JTPA Study', University of Chicago mimeo, November 1990.
Hoynes, Hilary and Thomas MaCurdy. 'Welfare Spells Over the Last Two Decades: Do Changes
    in Benefits Explain the Trends?', University of California, Berkeley mimeo, March 1993.
Hsiao, Cheng. Analysis of Panel Data, Cambridge University Press: Cambridge, 1986.
Hunter, John and Frank Schmidt. Methods of Meta-Analysis, Sage Publications: Newbury Park,
    1990.
Institute of Medicine, Preventing Low Birthweight, Washington D.C.: National Academy Press,
    1985.
Inter-University Consortium for Political and Social Research. Guide to Resources and
    Services 1992-1993, Ann Arbor MI, 1993.
Jargowsky, Paul and Mary Jo Bane. 'Ghetto Poverty: Basic Questions,' in Inner-City Poverty
    in the United States, Laurence Lynn and Michael McGeary (eds.), Washington D.C.:
    National Academy Press, 1990.
Jencks, Christopher et al. Inequality, New York: Basic Books, 1972.
Johnson, Gary. 'Rent Paying Ability and Racial Settlement Patterns: A Review and Analysis of
    Recent Housing Allowance Evidence,' American Journal of Economics and Sociology, 45
    #1, January 1986.
Jones, Jean Yavis. 'The WIC Program: Eligibility, Coverage, and Funding', Congressional
    Research Service, January 10, 1992.
Jones, Jean Yavis. 'Child Nutrition: Program Information, Funding and Participation FY 1980-
    FY 1990', Congressional Research Service, September 10, 1990.
Kain, John, 'A Universal Housing Allowance Program,' in Do Housing Allowances Work?
    Katharine Bradbury and Anthony Downs (eds.), Washington D.C.: The Brookings
    Institution, 1981.
Kehrer, Barbara and Charles Wolin. 'Impact of Income Maintenance on Low Birth Weight:
    Evidence from the Gary Experiment,' The Journal of Human Resources, XIV #4, 1979,
    434-462.

Kennedy, Eileen, Stanley Gershoff, Robert Reed and James Austin. 'Evaluation of the Effect of WIC Supplemental Feeding on Birth Weight.' *Journal of the American Dietetic Association, 80 #3*, March 1982.

Kennedy, Stephen and Merly Finkel. *Report of First Year Findings for the Freestanding Housing Voucher Demonstration*, Cambridge: ABT Associates, Inc. 1987.

Kerachsky, Stuart. 'Health and Medical Care Utilization: A Second Approach,' *The New Jersey Income Maintenance Experiment, Volume 3*, Harold Watts and Albert Rees (eds), New York: Academic Press, 1977.

Kisker, Ellen and Barbara Devaney. *The Food Choices of Low-Income Households*, Washington D.C.: Mathematica Policy Research, MPR Project # 7665-440, January 1988.

Korenman, Sanders and Jane Miller. *Food Stamp Program Participation and Maternal and Child Health*, Draft Report to the Food and Nutrition Service of the United States Department of Agriculture, May 1992.

Kotelchuck, Milton, Janet Schwartz, Marlene Anderka, and Karl Finison. 'WIC Participation and Pregnancy Outcomes: Massachusetts Statewide Evaluation Project.' *American Journal of Public Health, 74 #10*, October 1984.

Kozak, L.J. and E. McCarthy. 'Hospital Use by Children in the United States and Canada', *Vital and Health Statistics*, Series 5, No. (PHS)84-1477, Public Health Service, Washington D.C., August 1984.

Lalonde, Robert. 'Evaluating the Econometric Evaluations of Training Programs with Experimental Data,' *The American Economic Review, 76 #4*, September 1986, 604-620.

Lazere, Edward, Paul Leanard, Cushing Dolbeare, and Barry Zigas. *A Place to Call Home: The Low Income Housing Crisis Continues,* Washington D.C.: The Center on Budget and Policy Priorities, December 1991.

Lee, V.E., Brooks-Gunn, J., Schnur, E. 'Does Head Start Work? A 1-Year Follow-Up Comparison of Disadvantaged Children Attending Head Start, no Preschool, and other Pre school Programs,' *Developmental Psychology, 24*, 210-222, 1988.

Lee, Lung-Fei. 'Some Approaches to the Correction of Selectivity Bias', *Review of Economic Studies, 59*, 1982, 355-371.

Lefcowitz, Myron and David Elesh. 'Health and Medical Care Utilization,' *The New Jersey Income Maintenance Experiment, Volume 3*, Harold Watts and Albert Rees (eds), New York: Academic Press, 1977.

Leibowitz, Arleen, Marvin Eisen, and Winston Chow. 'An Economic Model of Teenage Pregnancy Decision-Making', *Demography, 23 #1*, Feb. 1986, 67-77.

Leibowitz, Arleen , W.G. Manning, E.B. Keeler, *et al.* 'Effect of Cost-Sharing on the Use of Health Services by Children: Interim Results from a Randomized Controlled Trial', *Pediatrics, 75*, 1985, 942-951.

Lerman, R. 'Do Welfare Programs Affect the Schooling and Work Patterns of Young Black Men?', in *The Black Youth Employment Crisis,* Richard Freeman and Harry Holzer (eds), Chicago: University of Chicago Press, 1986.

Long, Sharon. *The Impact of the School Nutrition Programs on Household Food Expenditures,* Washington D.C.: Mathematica Policy Research, October 30, 1987.

Lowry, Ira. *Experimenting with Housing Allowances: The Final Report of the Housing Assistance Supply Experiment,* Cambridge: Oelgeschlager, Gunn, and Hain, 1983.

Lundberg, Shelly and Robert Plotnick. 'Effects of State Welfare, Abortion and Family Planning Policies on Premarital Childbearing Among White Adolescents', *Family Planning Perspectives, 22 #6*, Nov./Dec. 1990, 246-252.

Lurie, Nicole. 'Preventive Care: Do We Practice What we Preach?,' *American Journal of Public Health, 77 #7*, July 1987, 801-804.

Maddala, G.S. *Limited-Dependent and Qualitative Variables in Econometrics*, Cambridge University Press: Cambridge, 1983.

Mallar, Charles. 'The Educational and Labor Supply Responses of Young Adults on the Urban Graduated Work Incentive Experiment,' *The New Jersey Income Maintenance Experiments,* Harold Watts and Albert Rees (eds), New York: Academic Press, 1977.

Manning, Willard, Joseph Newhouse, Naihua Duan, Emmett Keeler, Arleen Leibowitz, and Susan Marquis. 'Health Insurance and the Demand for Medical Care: Evidence from a Randomized Experiment,' *The American Economic Review,* June 1987, **77**, 251-277.

Markey, James. 'The Labor Market Problems of Today's High School Dropouts', *Monthly Labor Review,* June 1988, 36-43.

Marquis, Susan and Stephen Long. 'Uninsured Children and National Health Reform,' *Journal of the American Medical Association,* **268 #24**, December, 23/30, 1992, 3473-3477.

Marquis, Kent and Jeffrey Moore. 'Measurement Errors in the Survey of Income and Program Participation Program Reports', *Proceedings from the Sixth Annual Research Conference, Bureau of the Census,* 1990, 721-745.

Martorell, Reynaldo and Jean-Pierre Habicht, 'Growth in Early Childhood in Developing Countries', in *Human Growth: A Comprehensive Treatise,* F. Falkner and J. Tanner (eds.), 3, New York: Plenum Press, 1986.

Massachusetts Department of Health, Division of Family Health Services, *1983 Massachusetts Nutrition Survey,* Boston: Department of Health, October 1983.

Maurer, Kenneth. 'The National Evaluation of School Nutrition Programs: Factors Affecting Student Participation,' *The American Journal of Clinical Nutrition,* **40**, August 1984b, 425-447.

Maurer, Kenneth. 'The National Evaluation of School Nutrition Programs: Program Impact on Family Food Expenditures,' *The American Journal of Clinical Nutrition,* 40, August 1984a, 448-453.

Mayer, Susan and Christopher Jencks. 'The Social Consequences of Growing Up in a Poor Neighborhood,' in *Inner-City Poverty in the United States,* Laurence Lynn and Michael McGeary (eds.), Washington D.C.: National Academy Press, 1990.

Maynard, Rebecca and David Crawford. 'School Performance,' *Rural Income Maintenance Experiment: Final Report,* Madison WI: Institute for Research on Poverty, 1976.

Maynard, Rebecca and Richard Murnane. 'The Effects of Negative Income Tax on School Performance: Results of an Experiment,' *The Journal of Human Resources,* **XIV #4**, 1979.

McCormick *et al.* 'The Health and Development Status of Very-Low-Birth-Weight Children at School Age', *Journal of the American Medical Association,* **267**, 1992.

McDonald, M.S. and Monroe, E. *A Follow-up Study of the 1966 Head Start Program,* unpublished manuscript, Rome Georgia Public Schools, undated.

McKey, Ruth *et al. The Impact of Head Start on Children, Families and Communities: Final Report of the Head Start Evaluation, Synthesis and Utilization Project,* Washington D.C.: CSR, Incorporated, 1985.

McLanahan, Sara. 'Family Structure and Dependency: Early Transitions to Female Household Headship', *Demography,* **25**, February 1988, 1-16.

McLanahan, Sara, Nan Astone, and Nadine Marks. 'The Role of Mother-Only Families in Reproducing Poverty,' in *Children in Poverty,* Athetha Huston (ed), New York: Cambridge University Press, 1991.

Metcoff, Jack *et al.* 'Effect of Food Supplementation (WIC) During Pregnancy on Birth Weight.' *The American Journal of Clinical Nutrition,* **41**, May 1985.

Meyers, Alan, Amy Sampson, Michael Weitzman and Herb Kane. 'School Breakfast Program and School Performance', mimeo, Tufts University, May 1988.

Meyers, Alan *et al.* 'Public Housing Subsidies May Improve Poor Children's Nutrition,' *American Journal of Public Health,* **83 #1**, January 1993.

Miller, Jane and Sanders Korenman. 'Poverty, Nutrition Status, Growth and Cognitive Development of Children in the United States', Office of Population Research Princeton University, Working Paper #93-5, June 1993.

Mitchell, Janet and Rachel Schurman. 'Access to Private Obstetrics/Gynecology Services Under Medicaid,' *Medical Care*, **22**, November 1984, 1026-1037.

Moffitt, Robert. 'Incentive Effects of the U.S. Welfare System: A Review', *Journal of Economic Literature*, **30**, March 1992, 1-61.

Moffitt, Robert. 'Estimating the Value of an In-Kind Transfer: The Case of Food Stamps', *Econometrica*, **57#2**, March 1989, 385-410.

Moore, Kristin and Steven Caldwell. 'The Effect of Government Policies on Out-of-Wedlock Sex and Pregnancy', *Family Planning Perspectives*, **9 #4**, July/August 1977, 164-169.

Moss, Nancy and Karen Carver. 'Poverty, Welfare Program Participation and Infant Mortality in the United States,' mimeo, National Institute of Child Health and Human Development, Spring 1993.

Mulroy, Elizabeth. 'The Search for Affordable Housing,' in *Women as Single Parents: Confronting the Institutional Barriers in the Courts, the Workplace and the Housing Market*, E. Mulroy (ed.), New York: Auburn House, 1988.

Murray, Charles. *Losing Ground*, New York: Basic Books, 1984.

Murray, Michael. 'Subsidized and Unsubsidized Housing Starts: 1961-1977,' *Review of Economics and Statistics*, **65**, November 1983, 590-97.

National Governor's Association. 'State Coverage of Pregnant Women and Children — January 1990', mimeo, Washington D.C., 1990.

National Governor's Association. 'State Coverage of Pregnant Women and Children — January 1992', mimeo, Washington D.C., 1992.

National Center for Health Statistics, *Growth Charts*, Washington D.C.: Department of Health and Human Services, 1976.

Nelson, Charles and Richard Startz. 'The Distribution of the Instrumental Variables Estimator and its T-ratio When the Instrument is a Poor One,' *Journal of Business*, 63.1.2:S125-40, 1990a.

Nelson, Charles and Richard Startz. 'Some Further Results on the Exact Small Sample Properties of the Instrumental Variable Estimator', *Econometrica*, **58 #4**, July 1990b, 967-976.

Newey, Whitney. 'Efficient Estimation of Limited Dependent Variable Models', *Journal of Econometrics*, **36**, 1987, 231-250.

Newhouse, Joseph. 'Medical Care Costs: How Much Welfare Loss?' *Journal of Economic Perspectives*, **6 #3**, Summer 1992, 3-22.

Newman, Sandra and Ann Schnare. *Subsidizing Shelter, The Relationship Between Welfare and Housing Assistance*, Washington D.C.: Urban Institute Report 88-1, 1988.

O'Conner, Frank, Patrick Madden, and Allen Prindle. 'Nutrition,' *Rural Income Maintenance Experiment: Final Report*, Madison WI: Institute for Research on Poverty, 1976.

Owen, *et al.* 'Nutritional-Status of Preschool Children: Hemoglobin, Hematocrit, and Plasma Iron Values,' *Journal of Pediatrics*, **76(5)**:761, 1970.

Parker, Lynn. *The Relationship Between Nutrition and Learning*, Washington D.C.: National Education Association, 1989.

Pedone, Carla. *Current Housing Problems and Possible Federal Responses*, Washington D.C.: Congressional Budget Office, 1988.

Perloff, Janet. 'Health Care Resources for Children and Pregnant Women', *The Future of Children*, **2 #2**, Winter 1992.

Piper, J,M., W.A. Ray and M.R. Griffen. 'Effects of Medicaid Eligibility Expansion on Prenatal Care and Pregnancy Outcome in Tennessee', *Journal of the American Medical Association*, **264**, 1990, 2219-2223.

Plant, Mark. 'An Empirical Analysis of Welfare Dependence', *The American Economic Review,* **74 #4**, 1984, 673-684.

Poirier, Dale. 'The Determinants of Home Buying,' *The New Jersey Income Maintenance Experiment, Volume 3*, Harold Watts and Albert Rees (eds), New York: Academic Press, 1977.

Plotnick, Robert. 'Determinants of Teenage Out-of-Wedlock Childbearing', *Journal of Marriage and the Family,* **52**, 1990.

Poterba, James. 'Taxation and Housing: Old Questions, New Answers,' *The American Economic Review,* **82#2**, May 1992, 237-242.

Pozdena, Randall and Terry Johnson. 'Demand for Assets,' in *A Guaranteed Annual Income: Evidence From a Social Experiment*, New York: Academic Press, 1980.

Preston, Samuel. 'Children and the Elderly: Divergent Paths for America's Dependents,' *Demography,* **21 #4**, November 1984, 435-457.

Radzikowski, Jack and Steven Gale. 'Requirement for the National Evaluation of School Nutrition Programs,' *The American Journal of Clinical Nutrition,* **40**, August 1984a, 365-367.

Radzikowski, Jack and Steven Gale. 'The National Evaluation of School Nutrition Programs: Conclusions,' *The American Journal of Clinical Nutrition,* **40**, August 1984b, 454-461.

Rainwater, Lee. 'Class, Culture, Poverty and Welfare', Center for Human Resources, Heller Graduate School, mimeo, 1984.

Rein, Martin and Lee Rainwater, 'Patterns of Welfare Use', *Social Service Review,* 1978.

Reis, P. 'Health of Black and White Americans 1985-1987', Hyattsville MD: National Center for Health Statistics, Series 10 #171, 1990.

Reisinger, K.S. and J.A. Bires. 'Anticipatory Guidance in Pediatric Practice,' *Pediatrics* **66**, 1989, 889-1014.

Rosen, Harvey. 'Housing Behavior and the Experimental Housing-Allowance Program: What Have We Learned?' in *Social Experimentation*, Jerry Hausman and David Wise (eds.), Chicago: The University of Chicago Press, 1985.

Rosenbach, Margo. 'The Impact of Medicaid on Physician Use by Low-Income Children,' *American Journal of Public Health,* **79 #9**, September 1989, 1220-1226.

Rosenbaum, James, L.S. Rubinowitz, and M.J. Kulieke. *Low Income African-American Children in White Suburban Schools,* Evanston IL: Center for Urban Affairs and Policy Research, Northwestern University, 1986.

Rosenbaum, James. 'Black Pioneers – Do Their Moves to the Suburbs Increase Economic Opportunity for Mothers and Children?' *Housing Policy Debate,* **2 #4**, 1992, 1179-1213.

Rosenzweig, Mark and T. Paul Schultz. 'The Stability of Household Production Technology, A Replication', *The Journal of Human Resources,* **23**, Fall 1988, 535-549.

Rosenzweig, Mark and T. Paul Schultz. 'The Behavior of Mothers as Inputs to Child Health: The Determinants of Birth Weight, Gestation, and Rate of Fetal Growth', in *Economic Aspects of Health*, Victor Fuchs (ed) University of Chicago Press: Chicago, 1982.

Rosenzweig, Mark and T. Paul Schultz. 'Estimating a Household Production Function: Heterogeneity, the Demand for Health Inputs, and Their Effects on Birth Weight', *Journal of Political Economy,* **91**, October 1983, 723-46.

Rush, David. 'Evaluation of the Special Supplemental Food Program for Women, Infants and Children (WIC).' North Carolina: Research Triangle Institute, 1987.

Rydell, Peter, Kevin Neels, and Lance Barnett. *Price Effects of a Housing Allowance Program,* RAND Report R-2720-HUD, Santa Monica: The RAND Corporation, September 1982.

Rymer, Marilyn and Gerald Adler. 'Children and Medicaid: The Experience in Four States,' *Health Care Financing Review,* **9 #1**. Fall 1987, 1-20.

Sard, Barbara. 'The Role of the Courts in Welfare Reform,' *Women as Single Parents: Confronting Institutional Barriers in the Courts, the Workplace, and the Housing Market,* Elizabeth Mulroy (ed), New York: Auburn House, 1988.

Scholtz, John Karl. 'The Earned Income Tax Credit: Participation, Compliance, and Antipoverty Effectiveness,' Dept. of Economics, University of Wisconsin-Madison, mimeo, September 1993.

Schramm, Wayne. 'Prenatal Participation in WIC Related to Medicaid Costs for Missouri Newborns: 1982 Update.' *Public Health Reports*, **101 #6**, Nov.-Dec. 1986.

Schramm, Wayne. 'WIC Prenatal Participation: Cost/Benefit Analysis for Missouri 1985-86.' Paper presented at the American Public Health Association Meeting, October 1989.

Schramm, Wayne. 'WIC Prenatal Participation and its Relationship to Newborn Medicaid Costs in Missouri: A Cost/Benefit Analysis.' *American Journal of Public Health*, **75 #8**, August 1985.

Schwarz, Rachel. 'What Price Prematurity?', *Family Planning Perspectives*, **21 #4**, July/ August 1989, 170-174.

Senauer, Ben and Nathan Young. 'The Impact of Food Stamps on Food Expenditures: Rejection of the Traditional Model,' *American Journal of Agricultural Economics*, **68**, 1986, 37-43.

Slesnick, Daniel. 'Gaining Ground: Poverty in the Postwar United States', *Journal of Political Economy*, **101 #1**, February 1993, 1-38.

Sloan, Frank, Janet Mitchell and Jerry Cromwell. 'Physician Participation in State Medicaid Programs,' *The Journal of Human Resources*, **13**, 1978, 211-245.

Smeeding, Timothy. *Cross National Perspectives on Trends in Child Poverty and the Effectiveness of Government Policies in Preventing Poverty among Families with Children in the 1980's: The First Evidence from LIS*, unpublished manuscript, 1989.

Smith, James P. and Finis Welch. 'Black Economic Progress After Myrdal,' *Journal of Economic Literature*, **XXVII**, June 1989, 519-564.

Smolensky, Eugene, Eirik Evenhouse and Siobhan Reilly. *Welfare Reform in California*, Berkeley CA: University of California, Berkeley, Institute of Governmental Studies Press, 1992.

Solon, Gary. 'Intergenerational Income Mobility in the United States', *The American Economic Review*, June 1992.

Solon, Gary, Mary Corcoran, Robert Gordon, and Deborah Laren. 'Sibling and Intergenerational Correlations in Welfare Program Participation', *The Journal of Human Resources*, **23** (Summer), 1988, 388-396.

Solon, Gary, Mary Corcoran, Robert Gordon, and Deborah Laren. 'A Longitudinal Analysis of Sibling Correlations in Economic Status', *The Journal of Human Resources*, Summer 1991.

St. Peter, R., P. Newacheck and N. Halfon. 'Access to Care for Poor Children: Separate and Unequal?,' *Journal of the American Medical Association*, 267:20, May 27, 1992, 2760-2764.

Staiger, Douglas and James Stock. 'Asymptotics for Instrumental Variables Regressions with Weakly Correlated Instruments,' The Kennedy School of Government Harvard University, mimeo, July 1993.

Starfield, Barbara. *Effectiveness of Medical Care: Validating Clinical Wisdom*, Baltimore: Johns Hopkins University Press, 1985.

Starfield, B. 'Motherhood and Apple Pie: The Effectiveness of Medical Care for Children', *Millbank Memorial Fund Quarterly*, **63**, # 3, 1985.

Stewart, Anne. *Head Start: Funding Eligibility, and Participation*, CRS Report for Congress, July 22, 1992.

Struyk, Raymond and Marc Bendick. *Housing Vouchers for the Poor: Lessons from a National Experiment*, Washington D.C.: The Urban Institute Press, 1981.

Struyk, Raymond. 'Comment on William Apgar's 'Which Housing Policy is Best?'.' *Housing Policy Debate*, **1 #1**, 1991. 41-51.

The Washington Post. 'Vaccines Don't Reach Poor Children', Thursday June 17, 1993, Washington D.C., 8.

The White House, Office of the Press Secretary. 'Remarks by the President to the National Governor's Association Winter Session,' February 3, 1993.

Theil, Henri. *Principles of Econometrics,* New York: Wiley, 1971.

Thomas, Duncan, John Strauss and Maria-Helena Henriques. 'How Does Mother's Education Affect Child Height?', *The Journal of Human Resources,* **26** *#2*, Spring 1991, 183-211.

Thomas, Duncan. 'Like Father, Like Son,' Yale University mimeo, 1992.

U.S. Bureau of the Census, *Statistical Abstract of the United States,* various years.

U.S. Conference of Mayors. *The Continuing Growth of Hunger, Homelessness, and Poverty in America's Cities: 1986. A 26-City Survey,* Washington, D.C.: U.S. Conference of Mayors, 1986.

U.S. Congress, Office of Technology Assessement. *Healthy Children: Investing in the Future,* Washington D.C.: U.S. Government Printing Office (OTA-H-345), February 1988.

U.S. Department of Health and Human Services, Centers for Disease Control, Public Health Service, *CDC Analysis of Nutritional Indices for Selected WIC Participants,* FNS-176, June 1978.

U.S. Department of Health and Human Services, *Vital Statistics of the United States: Natality,* Washington D.C.: GPO, various years.

U.S. Department of Health and Human Services, Health Care Financing Administration, *State Medicaid Manual, #4,* July 1990.

U.S. Department of Agriculture, Food and Nutrition Service, *Evaluation of the Child Care Food Program,* Washington D.C.: USDA, 1983.

U.S. Department of Agriculture, Food and Nutrition Service, *Evaluation of the Summer Food Service Program Final Report,* Washington D.C.: USDA, August 1988.

U.S. General Accounting Office. 'Prenatal Care: Medicaid Recipients and Uninsured Women Obtain Insufficient Care,' Washington D.C.: U.S. Government Printing Office, 1985.

U.S. Health Care Financing Administration. *Medicare and Medicaid Data Book, 1986,* HCFA: Washington D.C., 1986.

U.S. Health Care Financing Adminstration. *Medicare and Medicaid Data Book, 1988,* HCFA:, Washington D.C., 1988.

U.S. House Select Commitee on Children, Youth and Families. *U.S. Children and their Families: Current Conditions and Recent Trends, 1989,* Report 101-356, Washington D.C.: U.S. Government Printing Office, 1989.

U.S. House of Representatives, Committee on Ways and Means. *Overview of Entitlement Programs: 1992 Green Book,* Washington D.C.: U.S. Government Printing Office, May 15, 1992.

U.S. House of Representatives Committee on Ways and Means. *1991 Green Book: Background Material and Data on Programs Within the Jurisdiction of the Committee on Ways and Means,* WMCP-102-9. Washington D.C.: U.S. Government Printing Office, May 1991.

Venti, Steven. 'The Effects of Income Maintenance on Work, Schooling, and Non-Market Activities of Youth,' *Review of Economics and Statistics,* February 1984, **66** *#1* 16-25.

Vermeersch, Joyce, Sally Hanes, and Steven Gale. 'The National Evaluation of School Nutrition Programs: Program Impact on Anthropometric Measures', *The American Journal of Clinical Nutrition,* **40,** August 1984, 414-424.

Vinovskis, Maris. 'Early Childhood Education: Then and Now,' *Daedalus,* **122** *#1,* 151-176, Winter 1993.

Waterlow, J., *et al.* 'The Presentation and Use of Height and Weight Data Comparing the Nutritional Status of Groups of Children under 10 Years Old,' *Bulletin of the World Health Organization,* **55**: 489-98, 1977.

Weicher, John. 'Comment on William Apgar's "Which Housing Policy is Best?" ' *Housing Policy Debate,* **1** *#1.* 1990, 33-40.

Welch, Finis. 'Black-White Differences in Returns to Schooling,' *The American Economic Review,* **63** *#5,* December 1973, 893-907.

Wellisch, Jean *et al. The National Evaluation of School Nutrition Programs: Final Report, Volume 1 – Overview and Presentation of Findings.* Santa Monica, CA: Systems Development Corporation, 1983a.

Wellisch, Jean *et al. The National Evaluation of School Nutrition Programs: Final Report, Volume 2 – Technical Appendices.* Santa Monica, CA: Systems Development Corporation, 1983b.

Wellisch, Jean and Lawrence Jordan. 'Sampling and Data Collection Methods in the National Evaluation of School Nutrition Programs,' *The American Journal of Clinical Nutrition,* **40**, August 1984, 368-381.

West, D.A. and D.W. Price. 'The Effects of Income, Assets, Food Programs, and Household Size on Food Consumption,' *American Journal of Agricultural Economics,* 1976, 725-730.

Westinghouse Learning Corporation and Ohio University, *The Impact of Head Start: An Evaluation of the Effects of Head Start on Children's Cognitive and Affective Development,* v.1 and 2, Report to the Office of Economic Opportunity, Athens, Ohio: WLC and Ohio State, 1969.

White, K. 'Efficacy of Early Intervention,' *Journal of Special Education,* **41**, 401-416, 1985-86.

Wilson, William Julius. *The Truly Disadvantaged,* Chicago: University of Chicago Press, 1987.

Wise, Paul and Alan Meyers. 'Poverty and Child Health,' *The Pediatric Clinics of North America,* **35 #6**, December 1988, 1169-1186.

Wood, David, Burciaga Valdez, Toshi Hayashi, and Albert Shen. 'Health of Homeless Children and Housed, Poor Children,' *Pediatrics,* **86 #6**, December 1990, 858-866.

Woodwell, David. *Office Visits to Pediatric Specialists, 1989,* Advance data from Vital and Health Statistics # 208, Hyattsville, MD: National Center for Health Statistics, 1992.

Woolridge, Judith. 'Housing Consumption,' in *The New Jersey Income Maintenance Experiment, Volume 3,* Harold Watts and Albert Rees (eds), New York: Academic Press, 1977.

Yelowitz, Aaron. 'The Medicaid Notch, Labor Supply and Welfare Participation: Evidence from Eligibility Expansions,' MIT mimeo, July 1993.

Yip, R., N.J. Binkin, I. Fleshood *et al.* 'Declining Prevalence of Anemia Among Low Income Children in the United States,' *Journal of the American Medical Association,* **258**, 1987, 1619-1623.

Yudkowsky, B.K., J.D. Cartland, and S.S. Flint. 'Pediatrician Participation in Medicaid: 1978-1989,' *Pediatrics,* **85 #4**, 1992, 567-577.

Zigler, W.E., W. Abelson, and V. Seitz. 'Motivational Factors in the Performance of Economically Disadvantaged Children on the PPVT', *Child Development,* **44**, 1973, 294-303.

Zill, Nicholas and Charlotte Schoeborn. National Center for Health Statistics. *Developmental Learning and Emotional Problems: Health of Our Nation's Children, United States 1988,* Vital and Health Statistics, # 190, November 16, 1990.

Zimmerman, David. 'Regression Towards Mediocrity in Economic Stature', *The American Economic Review,* June 1992.

Zimmerman, David and Phillip Levine. 'The Intergenerational Correlation in AFDC Participation: Welfare Trap or Poverty Trap', Williams College mimeo, April 1993.

DATA APPENDIX

TABLE 27
Some Data Sets Relevant to the Study of Child Well-Being

Data Set	Description
Owen's PNS, Owen's Preschool Nutritional Survey (1968–70)	A cross-sectional sample (Owen, Kram, Garry, *et al*, 1974) of preschool children in the US, with considerable individual socioeconomic, nutrition and health information. The survey was designed in order to compare subsets of the population, rather than oversampling poverty populations. 3,441 children from 74 sample areas in 36 states and the District of Columbia were sampled.
TSNS, Ten State Nutrition Survey (1968–70)	A survey by the Department of Health, Education and Welfare, under Congressional direction. Data were obtained on children in the lowest socioeconomic sections of ten states, by questionnaires and examinations. The survey contains over 80,000 individuals, with 12,000 children six years of age and below.
NHANES I, First National Health and Nutrition Survey (1971–75)	National Center for Health Statistics (NCHS) dataset. Oversampling of persons thought to be at high risk of malnutrition (persons with low incomes, preschool children, women of childbearing age, and the elderly). Included medical, eye and dental exams, and personal interviews. The survey contains 20,479 individuals, with 4,952 between the ages of one and eleven.
NHANES II, Second National Health and Nutrition Survey (1976–80)	NCHS dataset, similar to NHANES I. Oversampled children and low income population. The survey contains 20,322 individuals, with 7,011 between the ages 6 months and 17 years.
HHANES (1982–84)	NCHS dataset, similar to NHANES, but conducted on a nationwide probability sample of 16,000 eligible Hispanics.
NDB, National Nutrition Data Bank (ongoing)	Databank maintained by the US Department of Agriculture which stores nutrient data for an ever expanding array of foods. Information from the NDB is published in the USDA Agricultural Handbook, no. 8, which has several thousand entries and is constantly augmenting. The NDB is used by many studies in order to translate from food available to nutrients available.

TABLE 27 (Continued)

Data Set	Description
NFCS-LI, Low Income Supplement to the Nationwide Food Consumption Survey (1977–78)	The USDA sampled 4,400 low-income housekeeping households (those with at least one person having 10 or more meals from household food supplies during the 7 days preceding the interview). Provides detailed information on household food use, broken into household and individual data. Was taken before the elimination of the purchase requirement (EPR) in the Food Stamp Program.
SFC-LI, Survey of Food Consumption in Low Income Households (1979–80)	The USDA sampled 2,900 low-income housekeeping households eligible to receive Food Stamp Program benefits. The objective of the SFC-LI was to obtain information on changes in food use and dietary adequacy that were associated with increasing food prices and the EPR.
CSS, Cross-Sectional Survey of Students (1980)	Field study conducted for the National Evaluation of School Nutrition Programs. Designed to provide nationally representative sample of public school students in grades 1 to 12. Survey of students and teachers; oversamples students in poorer school districts. The survey contains 6,566 students.
HSP, Household Survey of Parents (1980)	Field study conducted for the National Evaluation of School Nutrition Programs. Compliments the CSS by surveying families of the 6,566 children participating in CSS.
FAS, Food Administrator Survey (1981)	Field study conducted for the National Evaluation of School Nutrition Programs, involving mail surveys of state, district, and school food service administrators. Compliments CSS and HSP, by surveying 848 school districts where CSS children are enrolled. 1,107 schools were surveyed.
NFCS-CSFII, Nationwide Food Consumption Survey, Continuing Survey of Food Intakes by Individuals (1985, 1986, 1989)	A longitudinal survey of US households by the USDA that contain one or more women from 19 to 50 years of age. Household participation lasts for one year in which a 24-hours dietary recall is administered six times at two-month intervals. Over 2,000 households with over 1,300 children between one and five years of age were surveyed.

TABLE 27 (Continued)

Data Set	Description
NFCS, Nationwide Food Consumption Survey (1987 – 88)	The USDA oversampled 3,600 low-income housekeeping households, providing detailed information on their household food use broken into household and individual data. The sample was after the EPR and can be compared with the SFC-LI as it was also conducted post-EPR.
CDC-PNSS, Center for Disease Control-Pediatric Nutrition Surveillance System (1983, 1986)	Two surveys done by the Center for Disease Control. The first, in 1983, collected data on 539,322 children from birth to 9 years of age. The children were all enrolled in public food and/or health programs. The 1986 survey reported data on over 800,000 children under 60 months of age.
PSID, Panel Study of Income Dynamics (1968– present)	A panel survey put out by the Survey Research Council of Michigan. Children born after 1968 and members of sample families that have split off to form new households are also tracked. Surveys of households take place every year and are most often done by telephone. Approximately 20,000 people are currently responding to this survey. The PSID oversamples the poor.
SIPP, Survey of Income and Program Participation (1984 – present)	A panel survey done by the Bureau of the Census, designed to improve imformation on the income distribution and well-being of the population, and on participation and eligibility for a wide range of government social welfare programs. Surveys of anywhere from 12,000 to 20,000 households take place every four months for two and a half years.
CES, Consumer Expenditure Survey (1979 – present)	A quarterly survey conducted by the Bureau of Labor Statistics which contains a detailed account of consumption patterns, family characteristics, individual assets and income from different sources. The survey contains highly disaggregated classes of commodities. Over 5,000 US households are surveyed each month.

TABLE 27 (Continued)

Data Set	Description
CPS, Current Population Survey (1968 – present)	A monthly survey conducted for the Bureau of Labor Statistics by the Bureau of the Census. Houses are interviewed month to month for 4 months, and then again for the corresponding time period a year later. Each monthly CPS has standard questions plus particular topics of interest for that month. The March CPS, for instance, is the Annual Demographic file, and contains all the basic demographic data for the households for that year. Approximately 58,000 households are surveyed each month.
VSCP, Vital Statistics Cooperative Program (1968 – present)	A monthly ongoing data system produced by the National Center for Health Statistics (NCHS). Contains general natality, mortality, marriage and divorce data, which is obtained from birth, death, marriage and divorce certificates. For almost all years, the sample includes every birth and death certificate in the US that year, and a sample of one in five of the marriage and divorce certificates.
Linked Birth/Infant Death Program (1983 – 1986)	NCHS dataset with two distinct files, (1) the numerator file comprised of linked birth and infant death statistical records; and (2) the denominator file, which contains NCHS natality statistical records. Links infant death with parental and infant statistical information. The numerator file alone has close to 40,000 records each year.
NNS, National Natality Survey (1974 – 69, 1972, 1980)	NCHS dataset constructed by surveys which follow back on one or more informants identified on vital records. Contains surveys of parents, physicians and hospitals. Four NNS datasets exist, while the NMIHS serves as a fifth, in that it covers the same information in 1988. The sample contains anywhere from 3,000 to 10,000 records per year.
NIMS, National Infant Mortality Survey (1964 – 66)	NCHS dataset constructed similarly to the NNS, but contains multiple records per sample child for a sample total of 7,800 records.
NFMS, National Fetal Mortality Survey (1980)	Combined with the 1980 NNS to extend the scope of questions asked. Contains 16,327 records.
NMIHS, National Maternal and Infant Health Survey (1988)	The equivalent of a 1988 NNS, 1988 NIMS and 1988 NFMS survey, Vital records tapes are linked with 19,000 mothers' questionnaires. Contains information on live births, fetal deaths, and infant deaths.

JANET CURRIE

Data Set	Description
NHIS, National Health Interview Survey (1969 – 90)	NCHS dataset constructed by weekly surveys of the US civilian noninstitutionalized population, conducted in households. Obtains information on each member of the household. Five posssible record types: health condition, doctor visits, hospital stays, household characteristics, and person characteristics. The survey contains 36,000 to 47,000 households and 92,000 to 125,000 individuals per year. Supplements in 1981 and 1988 pertain to children.
NHIS-CH, National Health Interview Survey on Child Health (1988)	NCHS dataset which was an extension of the 1988 NHIS. Questionnaire asked additional questions all pertaining to children's health, educational attainment and behavioral problems. The survey covers 17,000 children up to the age of 17.
NSFG, National Survey of Family Growth (1973, 1976, 1982, 1988)	NCHS dataset constructed by personal and telephone interviews of mothers 15–44 years of age. Provides information on pregnancy, contraception, marital status, use of family planning services. Has separate information corresponding to each of the woman's pregnancies. Sample size ranges from 7,900 to 9,800 women each year.
NSHSPE, National School Health Services Program Evaluation (1981 – 1982)	This survey documents the nature and scope of a wide range of health service provided to school age children by nurse practioners, school health nurses, physicians, and health aides. Data are supplied for school health programs at a total of 30 schools at six sites in the US by a parent questionnaire and a medical history and practitioner questionnaire. (Freeman, Howard and Robert J. Meeker)
NAEP, National Assessment of Educational Progress (1970 – 1980)	A survey by the Education Commission of the States, which attempts to measure different learning areas taught in school by testing children aged 5 to 17. Each year 75,000 to 100,000 students were tested , in the process of making a multistage probability sample.
HSB, High School and Beyond (1980, 1982, 1986)	A multi-cohort longitudinal survey conducted by the National Opinion Research Center for the National Center for Education Statistics. High school sophomores and seniors are interviewed, along with parents, teachers and high school principals. The initial sample in 1980 included 58,270 students,

TABLE 27 (Continued)

Data Set	Description
	(28,240 seniors and 30,030 sophomores). The sophomore cohort portion of the follow up replicates nearly all the tests done in the base year, while the senior cohort portion emphasizes postsecondary education and work experiences.
NLSY, National Longitudinal Survey of Youth (1979 – present)	A survey which began in 1979 with over 12,000 young people between the ages of 14 and 21. These subjects have been reinterviewed every year since. Conducted by the Center for Human Resource Research at Ohio State University, Participants answer questions about work history, household composition, fertility, education, etc. Some background information about the respondents' parents is also available.
NLSCM, National Longitudinal Survey's Child-Mother file (1986, 1988, 1990)	A survey of the children of the National Longitudinal Survey of Youth (NLSY), by the Center for Human Resource Research at Ohio State University. Mothers are participants of the ongoing NLSY. Mothers answer questions concerning their children's schooling attainment, and utilization of health care. Children completed age-appropriate assessments of cognitive skills. African-Americans, Hispanics, and the poor are oversampled, with a sample size of 6,283 mothers and 8,500 children, including many sibling pairs.
MF-CSLVY, Monitoring the Future: A Continuing Study of the Lifestyles and Values of Youth (1976 – 89)	Annual surveys of high school seniors designed to quantify the direction and rate of change in teen attitudes over time. Each year 16,000 to 19,000 students are surveyed in public and private high schools. (Bachman, Johnston, and O'Malley)
NYS, National Youth Survey (1976 – 80)	This dataset was supported by the Center for Studies of Crime and Delinquency, National Institute of Mental Health, the National Institute for Juvenile Justice and Delinquency Prevention, and later by the Bureau of Justice Statistics. Close to 2,000 parent and youth cases are surveyed each year, asking questions pertaining to the year just passed.
NSC, National Survey of Children (1976, 1981, 1987)	A cross section dataset in 3 waves asking questions pertaining to child's well-being, lifestyle, development and family experience. The survey includes 1,400 to 2,300 children between the ages of 7 and 11.

TABLE 27 (Continued)

Data Set	Description
NCS-CSS, National Crime Surveys Crime School Supplement (1989)	Supplement to the National Crime Survey by the US Dept. of Justice, Bureau of Justice Statistics. 15,353 students 12 years of age and above were surveyed. The National Crime Surveys contain national data concerning all types of crimes and demographics on victims and perpetrators.
American Housing Survey (annually through 1970s, 1983, 1989)	A periodic survey of the housing conditions of households in a specific set of American cities. Contains detailed information about housing conditions, rents, mobility, and demographic composition of households. Available from HUD.

Sources: Further information about most of these data sets is available in ICPSR (1993). For information about the Owen's Preschool Nutrition Survey see Owen *et al.* (1970).For information about the Ten State Nutrition Survey see Garn and Clark (1975). See Wellisch and Jordan (1984) for information about the CSS, HSP, and FAS. Contact the US Department of Agriculture, Human Nutrition Information Service, 6506 Bellcrest Rd., Rm. 338, Hyattsville MD 20782, (phone 301-436-8485) for further information about the NFCS-LI, NFCS, SFC-LI, and NDB. For the CDC-PNSS contact the US National Center for Health Statistics, Scientific and Technical Information Branch, 3700 East-West Highway, Hyattsville, MD 20782, (phone 301-436-8500).

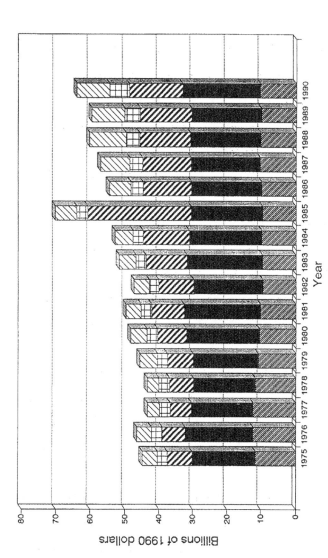

Note: The bulge in outlays in 1985 is caused by a change in the method of financing public housing, which generated close to $14 billion in one-time expenditures. This amount paid off-all at once-the capital cost of public housing construction and modernization activities undertaken between 1974 and 1985, which otherwise would have been paid off over periods of up to 40 years. Because of this one-time expenditure, however, future outlays for public housing will be lower than they would have been otherwise.

FIGURE 14 Federal welfare expenditures

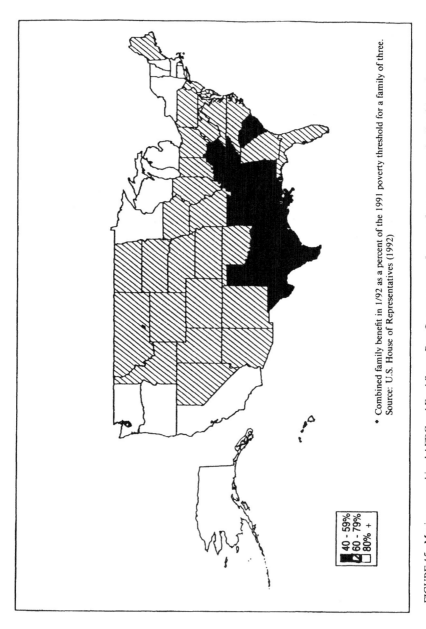

FIGURE 15   Maximum combined AFDC and Food Stamp Benefit as a percent of poverty for a one-parent family of three, January 1992*

* Combined family benefit in 1/92 as a percent of the 1991 poverty threshold for a family of three.
  Source: U.S. House of Representatives (1992)

40 - 59%
60 - 79%
80% +

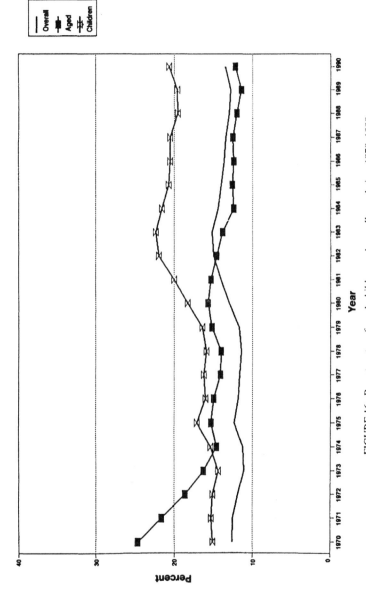

FIGURE 16 Poverty rates of aged, children and overall population, 1970–1990.

Source: U.S. House of Representatives (1992)

Index

FUNDAMENTALS OF PURE AND APPLIED ECONOMICS

SECTIONS AND EDITORS

BALANCE OF PAYMENTS AND INTERNATIONAL FINANCE
W. Branson, Princeton University
DISTRIBUTION
A. Atkinson, London School of Economics
ECONOMIC DEVELOPMENT STUDIES
S. Chakravarty, Delhi School of Economics
ECONOMIC HISTORY
P. David, Stanford University, and M. Lévy-Leboyer, Université
Paris X
ECONOMIC SYSTEMS
J.M. Montias, Yale University
ECONOMICS OF HEALTH, EDUCATION, POVERTY AND
CRIME
V. Fuchs, Stanford University
ECONOMICS OF THE HOUSEHOLD AND INDIVIDUAL
BEHAVIOR
J. Muellbauer, University of Oxford
ECONOMICS OF TECHNOLOGICAL CHANGE
F.M. Scherer, Harvard University
EVOLUTION OF ECONOMIC STRUCTURES, LONG-TERM
MODELS, PLANNING POLICY, INTERNATIONAL ECONOMIC
STRUCTURES
W. Michalski, O.E.C.D., Paris
EXPERIMENTAL ECONOMICS
C. Plott, California Institute of Technology
GOVERNMENT OWNERSHIP AND REGULATION OF
ECONOMIC ACTIVITY
E. Bailey, Carnegie-Mellon University, USA
INTERNATIONAL ECONOMIC ISSUES
B. Balassa, The World Bank
INTERNATIONAL TRADE
M. Kemp, University of New South Wales

LABOR AND ECONOMICS
F. Welch, Texas A&M University, Texas, USA
MACROECONOMIC THEORY
J. Grandmont, CEPREMAP, Paris
MARXIAN ECONOMICS
J. Roemer, University of California, Davis
NATURAL RESOURCES AND ENVIRONMENTAL ECONOMICS
C. Henry, Ecole Polytechnique, Paris
ORGANIZATION THEORY AND ALLOCATION PROCESSES
A. Postlewaite, University of Pennsylvania
POLITICAL SCIENCE AND ECONOMICS
J. Ferejohn, Stanford University
PROGRAMMING METHODS IN ECONOMICS
M. Balinski, Ecole Polytechnique, Paris
PUBLIC EXPENDITURES
P. Dasgupta, University of Cambridge
REGIONAL AND URBAN ECONOMICS
R. Arnott, Boston College, Massachusetts
SOCIAL CHOICE THEORY
A. Sen, Harvard University
STOCHASTIC METHODS IN ECONOMIC ANALYSIS
Editor to be announced
TAXES
R. Guesnerie, Ecole des Hautes Etudes en Sciences Sociales, Paris
THEORY OF THE FIRM AND INDUSTRIAL ORGANIZATION
A. Jacquemin, Université Catholique de Louvain

FUNDAMENTALS OF PURE AND APPLIED ECONOMICS

PUBLISHED TITLES

For Product Safety Concerns and Information please contact our
EU representative GPSR@taylorandfrancis.com Taylor & Francis
Verlag GmbH, Kaufingerstraße 24, 80331 München, Germany